GW01179759

POETRY now

In The Shadows

Edited by

Heather Killingray

First published in Great Britain in 2004 by
POETRY NOW
Remus House,
Coltsfoot Drive,
Peterborough, PE2 9JX
Telephone (01733) 898101
Fax (01733) 313524

SB ISBN 1 84460 860 3

FOREWORD

Although we are a nation of poets we are accused of not reading poetry, or buying poetry books. After many years of listening to the incessant gripes of poetry publishers, I can only assume that the books they publish, in general, are books that most people do not want to read.

Poetry should not be obscure, introverted, and as cryptic as a crossword puzzle: it is the poet's duty to reach out and embrace the world.

The world owes the poet nothing and we should not be expected to dig and delve into a rambling discourse searching for some inner meaning.

The reason we write poetry (and almost all of us do) is because we want to communicate: an ideal; an idea; or a specific feeling. Poetry is as essential in communication, as a letter; a radio; a telephone, and the main criterion for selecting the poems in this anthology is very simple: they communicate.

Contents

Love

Love is all around when we look around
Love is so special like your mum and dad
Sometimes love is like raindrops falling
Falling down from Heaven when the thunder
Stops, love is doing things that you should do.
Love is about sharing, not forgetting, caring
And cuddling late at night in candlelight.

Love is a smile from beautiful white teeth
Love is a chuckle from your heart
Love has a funny start, love is something
Not to be forgotten, it must live on
Let's all go round starry-eyed.

Love is seeing a baby smile, love is a
Little love bite on you neck, love is
Sharing a juicy steak, we must keep
This love thing going it's meant
For you and me.

Maddie Reade

A Good Name

Our parents gave to us a name, in this
we had no say,
We carry it with us all our life,
until our dying day.
Your name may be important, it may
even be quite small,
But it's how you make yourself matter
most of all.
For a name's worth more than riches
even gold or silver too.
For it can bring you loving favour
which the others cannot do,
It can give the joy of friendship for
without our friends we are lost.
So a good name's worth protecting
and we should not count the cost,
So if a thoughtless person ever says to you
Your name is not important,
that simply will not be true.

Sylvia Quayle

Finding Love

Looking in the mirror
what do I see?
A face with no expression
I'm just looking, it's me.

There's no one to love
in my life right now
I feel really empty
I've love to share.

Where is the man
I need by my side?
I've looked, I can't find him
I've really tried.

Where do I look
every avenue covered.
Maybe he's nearby
waiting to be discovered.

If I find my man
I'll hold on to him tight,
and make him my partner
for the rest of my life.

Then when I look in the mirror
my expression I'll see
will be happy, contented
as I used to be.

Joan Marrion

Sleep, My Lover

Sleep comes to claim me,
Drifting . . . melting . . . into nothing.

Oh sweet cousin of death, take me!
Kiss me with your liquid tongue,
Dissolve me in your velvet embrace

Swirling . . . sinking . . . lightness of being.

Welcome darkness enfolds,
I surrender completely -
Sub-conscious bliss, I am yours and you are mine.

Belinda Abraham

A Heaven's Treat

Burning light
Burning bright
In the midst of air
Appearing naked, bare
Dancing with heavenly joy.
Oh, what do I see now!
A manifestation of a sweet and humble boy,
Resting on a cloud
Drunk by his pride
And proving it aloud.
Oh so soft a sight
A feather diving in the night
Playing blissfully with care
Briskly touching the air.

Panagiota A Rentezelas Mihalou

FROM BEHIND THE CAMERA

He wanted me to take their picture
but he wanted her to kiss
I saw they looked happy and with bliss

She did not want to kiss for the camera
'cause she was camera shy
but he got angry and said, 'Why?'

Then they started to argue
and he laughed at me and said I was dim
and I stared out across the rim

I thought she looked so pretty
from behind the lens where I stood
as pretty as pretty, just like a girl should

But he did not think so
and he cast me a nasty stare
and the rest, they did not seem to even care

My heart was filled with sadness
as they all seemed to have a part to play
and I was the camera with nothing to say

Their laughter was false and their smiles
were just playing a part
when I saw their sadness, it cut through my heart

But to look through the camera was all I could do
then he shouted at me and I felt real sad
and he looked at me as though I was mad

So I put down the camera
where I so wanted to stay
and picked up my things
and sadly walked away

Melanie Goode

Clock Rolls

I can see the dawn, my life I want to pawn, trade it in
for money I can use. Sell myself, put my body up for rent
and let the money roll in, abuse me, use myself, off you went.

The clock rolls on and on, like the dawning and setting of the sun,
the moon at its peak, it was full, just last week,
now the fading has fallen vastly as the frivolous moon
dances off stage, too soon.

Into the distance, on you go, looking back, off you go,
future awaits you.
A multicultured life, multicoloured, multiplies before you.
Opportunity. I will stay behind, carry on, rock on this Earth.
Don't pity me.

The clock rolls forward in time, following the daily line,
the routine. Clean, happy and never mean, sunshine beams
over your halo-head like a light bulb, following your move.
Perfection, angelic reflection.

Off you gallop. I watch the shadows across the road,
blackening with the night-time that has once again fallen into my life.
I look for the stars, for comfort, for you.
Nothing is there. The lights in my life are switched off,
and I fall into the darkness myself.

The clock rolls and I stay behind.
My batteries ran out as time progressed
and the other clocks around me ticked on, synchronised. I gather dust.

Josh 'Zach' Bramley

IDENTITY

Do what you will to me
Blind me so I cannot see
But while I have my identity
I am more than you'll ever be

Bind me up and pull the rope tight
I will not go without a fight
Though it may cost me all my might
I will not be overcome by fright

Tear my skin with the claws of a cat
Treat me like your front doormat
I don't know what you're playing at
But you won't get rid of me like that

You've cost me my dignity
You've physically wounded and bound me
But I still have my identity
You cannot take that away from me

I still have my identity
You cannot take that away from me
While I have my identity
I am more than you will ever be

Abi Smith

THE CROCUS GECKO LIZARDS MUCUS MEMBRANE MOON EYE

Eyes are shrines; Saturn is Mars,
Jupiter has no real desires,
Nitrogen has gone from space,
Oxygen is what we breathe,
We are plants without baby seeds,
Noisy tropical jungles connect with the eye of the gecko's hollowness,
which are songs to bless the empty chamber of our hearts.
As the chancellor of bellies feed on crocodiles,
Where the moon eyed prism glosses the inner hall of memories,
Dispatched across the land of lunar ceremonies,
Crossing gently on mountain tops of residual degeneration's,
Who are sparkling killing flies with no disguise,
On the paper winds of our morbid death,
Concur the fur of the rose garden's space.
For now Jupiter begins to work to resume the poisonous fumes
of a nasty lark,
Upon the bark less skies under a solar kite of the lizards crocus eating,
Which will focus on destroying the development
of Christ's brutal beating.
So the mucus membranes defoliate,
Where he foolishly ate and we begin to silently wait the wise
old mountain of a volcanic spy.
As we stare at him like bloodless mannequins,
Waiting once more for the sweet old rye,
When the plant folds inwards and eventually will die,
While we adventure in lie,
Both the sun and moon will dust and pry.
Our perching embrace to the moonlit eye,
With his welcoming face to the wallowing spy.

John Hogan

He's Different

Our world is free and we're all proud
That all men walk this earth as equals,
But are we all really free?
Or is this just a myth
That we'd like to be true?

Look at him, what do you see?
A man, a human
Or the colour of his skin?
Yes, the first thing you see
Is black, white, yellow, brown.
He's different.

Does it stop there?
This man here, do you see him first,
Or the wheelchair on which he sits?
Yes, the first thing you see
Is the chair and the scars.
He's different.

Now look at this man before you
Do you see his pride and his self respect,
Or the clothes in which he stands?
Yes, the first thing you see
Is his rags of the road.
He's different.

Of course we aren't prejudice,
We're equal and free.
That's why half the world starves
While the other half feasts,
And why one half slaves
While the other lounges.

Linda Coulby

1804 - 2004

Rallying to the sound of the Lambi, they carved a path,
Through dusty streets they marched.
The women adorned in colourful aprons and headscarves,
The men, as if striving to follow soldier's past.
The old, sick, lame and the babies on wobbly legs,
A ragged bunch they looked, full of sorrows and woes,
Bearing on their faces, the determination of their ancestors.
The sweat and blood that nourished the slavers' soil,
Had turned poison in freedom's time, it seemed.
The God of the oppressors was the enemy, they felt,
Through countless years of indoctrination they learned
That He is merciful to friends and enemies alike.
Kneeling in their poverty-stricken churches,
They continue to praise Him, despite their obvious lack.
'Cause in their heart, they still believe
From all this chaos, their nation shall rise.
For theirs is a loving God, who will not always remain angry,
But will some day cause the bloody curse to depart forever.

Gladys Bruno

My Quest For You

I dream of treasures;
but I despise wealth and fame.
I want to be your conqueror,
without the subjugating sword.

I let your oceanic waves
Steer my caravel through the storms;
from dead mist to unknown waters,
until I arrive at you - my New World.

Woman,
you are a constant enigma,
the land of my hopes; I see you,
and I name you - San Salvador.
The desire of exploring you,
to make my own maps;
it is perpetual hunger calling
to venture myself beyond your shores.

I go over mountains,
and slowly descend into your valleys
with captivating forest.
Your exotic sweetness floods my senses;
I find the secret roads to your golden cities,
I bathe in the fluidity of your sensual rivers,
I feel the power of your volcanic areas
and your seasons.

Llangka

Wild Autumn

Leaves brittle crunch
under silent soled boots,
branches stripped bare
stark wait for
winter's raw bitter blast
of icy pure snow.

Trees lament
pause
wait patient
while nature's rhythmic
pattern prepared for spring.

Carole Taylor

Thro' The Gate

Spectre death all souls doth claim
Cheap is life yet longevity most aim
Existence transient each day
Consider our world's endangered pathway
Pause, take not for granted, ponder
Marvel our solar system's wonder
We could lose that all
Meteor collision, or by mans' dread fall
Alone in the eternal scheme we are as nought
Neither vanity nor conceit elevate us one whit by thought
'Self is the citadel,' 'tis said
Human spiritual Donjon if correctly read
Humbly realise our worth
Coursing life steadfastly forth
Accept in faith inevitable Nemesis fate
Enter, then, with hope, future's ever open gate.

C Harkness

MAP OF LIFE

I lied, I joked
I slandered His name

I fought, I cursed
I scared and I caused pain

He opened His arms
And beckoned me in
He showed me a world I could believe in

He made me free
He gave me forgiveness
He stretched out His arms
And cried
'Believe in this!'

He has drawn an
Exquisite map,
A map of my life
And beneath it my slogan will read

'I am an expression of the life of Christ,
Because Christ is my life.'

Bethany Meakin

A HEART AND A LUNG

Impelling every inspiration, drunken from this veneration
Inconspicuous enchasement of my secret bronchi basement
(You inebriate a lung . . . the other one's just highly strung)
The moment that I drink you in, a sigh expels you out again
So breathing is, I must confess, such pulmonary wastefulness.

Alas! Beneath the pounding drum of my pericardium
There you are as stimulation for my soft ventriculation
(My atria are almost free of anything you shouldn't see
Though even garnered love is wise, exposed by contumacious eyes)
When thoughts of you bring swift arrest, a heart can only do its best.

Here it is for all to see, you're fused to my biology
No mask to cloak or camouflage my discreet cellular homage
This body is iniquitous, of common sense contemptuous
A corporeal guile so strong, I dare not contemplate for long,
The side effects of revelation (should I tell you of my adoration?)

Johanna Widdowson

FADE AWAY

I try and try to be someone else
Someone, anyone
With good mental health
The loneliness is cold
As I give into the depression
The pain and fear
Lingers like a deep, dark confession
I want to be here
I want to grow old
But how can I?
When to myself I've been told
My death will be my happiness
My chance to be free
To give back the lives I've destroyed
Of the people I call my family
As I slowly fade away, day by day, by day.

Rachel Price

WHEN FATE PLAYS ITS GAME

When clouds of grief seem to be burgeoning,
And over the remnants of mindless ecstasy so ruthlessly spreading;
When every sliver of hope is ordained to be slaughtered,
And every breath of hope is dispassionately murdered -
Then in the vagaries of life one can hear,
Diabolic mirth laughing raucously at his passion to persevere.
Every beat from a failed heart, painfully phrasing;
Bitter wisdom to the vagabond so hopeful and trusting,
Still unknown to the heartless lashings by fate in life's mart
Where every thread bound to life is doomed to part.
Forbidding his delirium in beholding the same,
Because he will be scorned when fate plays its game.

Smita Ghatak

TWELVE STEPS TO SERENITY

There are twelve steps to happiness and I'll put them to the test, by starting with day one and giving alcohol a rest.

Day two is a must, I'm so full of grief, help me Dear Lord to have some belief!

Day three I'm in pain and I'm paying the bill, but with your guidance I'll do Your will.

Day four I look back at the times I was p****d. Lord help me remember and I'll make a list.

Day five is even harder for me to bear, came to believe that I care. With your help Dear Lord to find another to share.

Day six I am ready, if You'll grant me release, so that I may move forward, with calm and some peace.

Day seven is a mixture, I trip and I stumble. Please help me my Lord to let me be humble.

Day eight at last, so that I may look at my past, know the harm that I've done and do not pretend, for now I am willing to make my amends.

Day nine is here, let me be wise in my choice and hope these people hear my voice, for I'll do my best and leave the rest - for I do not want to hurt.

Day ten is for me so that I may see what I'm doing to others and also to me. Help me admit my wrongs in such a way so that I may do it in one day.

Day eleven I pray in peace and quiet and not shout, to know Your will and carry it out.

Day twelve has arrived and I hope I have learned that the gift of today is not to be spurned. You have taught me to live and all in a day. Lord let me be so humble as to give it away.

Peter Cranswick

Granny's Advice

Isn't it strange how sometimes we find,
The silliest things creep into our mind.
The latest thing to pop into my head
Is what my dear grandmother said.

'My girl' she said, 'now don't you forget
If you beget kindness then kindness you'll get.
If you beget love, then love will find you,
And always make sure you are honest and true.

For if you are not, then remember my pet,
It will come back to haunt you, so don't you forget.
Remember not all are as strong as you dear,
So give them a hand and show that you care.'

So I looked at the spider and had to decide,
Shall I flush him away or take him outside.
I smiled as I thought of Granny's advice,
And placed him outside, to continue his life.

Kathleen Paddon

In Search Of Truth

Lying down in bed
I close my eyes
close them hard
and my hand reaches out
(for my life)

a sign of a teardrop
makes my eye wet
but it won't fall
not yet

I stretch my arm
the tear dries out
but I can still feel it
a sudden deep breath
as I realise I still need it

the strain from the eyes disappears
slowly my eyes open as I turn my head
I look at my arm fallen towards the ground
and I hear it say, 'Not yet'

I open my mouth
the lungs fill with air
my eyes close again
am I still not there?

Karan Takulia

BROKEN METAPHOR

I removed my heart.
Pinned it out on a specimen tray,
dissected it where it lay.
Looking for wonder or art,
rhyme, reason.
Confusing the metaphysical
with the empirical,
I looked for love
in its hollow chambers.
Found only reminders
of you in its scarlet hues.
Hot blood now cool
in its ruptured core.

Nothing more.

Recalling beats
in synchonicity,
skin in seamless unity.
Nights blind in wonder
I squandered soulful words,
plundered swathes of starlit sky.
Evoked them in you eyes.
Every fibre of being
seeing, feeling, hearing you.
Symbolising faith restored,
you were worshipped, adored.
Gave you the world and more
with this broken metaphor.

Nothing more.

It's only flesh and blood.
What good is to anyone?
I left it there in public glare
for all to stop, stare.
Did not care anymore
who saw this travesty,
in all its broken majesty.
That used to pump confusion
Feed oxygen to delusion.
I'll donate it to the cynics,
consider cryogenics.
Let the present age ignore
why this heart still yearns

so much more.

Graham Collett

THE BALLERINA

Two long legs of suppleness and strength
Meet two ribboned feet at the end of their length
A nimble figure upon silken foot
With pointed toe sprite limbs are put
In the wind a graceful flower
Jetes commanding a wilful power
Up to the skies to the powder white cloud
A neck long and swan-like, holds a head high and proud
Elegance and athleticism bedecked in pearls
In a swift movement a flower unfurls
Leaves flutter softly and fall to the ground
The flower then dies and petals scatter around
Wafting in a circle her skirt brushes the floor
Born to a new life the flower is no more
Up she jumps on two wooden toes
Upwards a bird flies skyward it goes

Anita Maina Kulkarni

Skint Poet

Some day I'll write a poem
That will bring me lots of cash
I enter lots of contests
'Well you've got to have a bash'

But it's pay me this and pay me that
And we will print your work
Do they think I am round the bend
Or just some kind of jerk

One day I will write a poem!
That they'll all pay me lots to print
But until that wonderful day arrives
I'll have to be a poet, that's skint

D T Baker

Inside His Mind

His neglected newspapers lay on the floor,
He wouldn't be needing them anymore,
Not where he was going or where he had gone,
After all the good he'd done, he only did one wrong.
A drunken state, not himself
Put him in a jail cell with no one to help.
He sits and prays beneath the windows,
So little light let in at all,
His bones and body so frail and fragile
Why did he do it?
Why did he fall?
This would be the end of him,
He'd never be the same,
His simpleton habits gone at a blink,
His once detailed imagination, plain.
His hands trembled violently,
As he sat down to eat.
The others were scary and not to be mixed with,
So he stared down at his feet.
His devastation of what happened,
Filled his thoughts and dreams.
Everyone sees things through their eyes,
Nothing is as it seems.
Wrecked someone's life,
Taken it away,
Wouldn't be able to sleep at night,
Or think straight in the day.
But that's just the way things are,
It's not every day you hit a child with a car.
Don't drink drive, it wrecks lives.

Rehana Allison (14)

VOICES

We are the candle full of sinners; let us burn the world,
We are the world's source of imagination, let us be inspired,
We are glints in the fabric of ourselves, let us be torn
Our children are our rays of sunshine; let us cast a shadow,
We are the future of mankind, let us be destroyed.
We must beware ourselves . . .

Madeline Grimshaw

Apparition

Lost soul left behind,
In the shadows of a room.
His voice speaks through your mind
Whispering through and through.

Feel the presence of the ghost
Touch the windows filled with frost
Communicate with the ones you love the most
At no matter what cost

Crack a joke if you must
Because of your discomfort
You distrust

But the apparition
Wasn't from your imagination
It was from your heart, where you cried
Where no one can say you lied.

Conor McGreevy

UNWANTED GOODS

Up in the attic we have a root,
things we don't want for a car boot.
There's the lamp from Aunt Mabel,
ornaments and a coffee table.
Memorabilia will all have to go,
It's quite sad, I know.
But, we are making a fresh start
With ultra modern and art

We filled the car and off we went,
excited as we paid the rent.
Not many people appeared that day,
our hopes were dashed I must say

The car boot didn't go at all well,
we struggled trying hard to sell.
Ah well, the lamp from Aunt Mabel
Looks well on the coffee table!

Maybe next year we'll give it another go,
we might be luckier, I do hope so.

Sheila Singleton

LOVER BOY

Soundlessly he walks through my dreams,
With his midnight dark hair and hypnotic blue eyes.
His captivating smile melts my heart, as he takes my hand.
We walk hand in hand through the Garden of Eden,
In the balmy moonlit night.
No sound can be heard but the rustling of the leaves on the breeze,
And the beating of our hearts.
He kisses me under a cherry blossom tree,
And whispers promises and words of love.
Then morning comes and he's gone.
Just one magical moment in time.

Julie Wealleans

Words Are Not Enough

The first time that I saw her face, I fell into her eyes,
Such beauty did I see in them, her all immortalised.
They captured me just like a naive moth around a flame,
And instantly I knew my life would never be the same.

Her flowing locks like rays of sunlight on a spider's trap,
So elegant like swaying blades of grass infused with sap.
I longed to touch her perfect face, to stroke her yielding skin,
To gently kiss her blushing cheek, to touch her soul within.

Her faultless lips I yearned to utter forth such words so sweet,
Their melody a gentle wind to sweep me off my feet.
A single kiss I ached to grasp, to prove that she was real,
To close my eyes and hope her secrets to me she'd reveal.

Her body, so magnificent. A perfect paradigm,
I craved that one day she would me bestow her form, sublime.
And though she is not perfect, in my eyes she just could be,
If only you could look through mine, I know you would agree.

Her beauty and her talent rare, amazing like a dream,
I'll keep my fingers crossed one day our pathways will convene.
And though she knows not who I am, or that I do exist,
One day my heart will fly to her, so hopeless to resist.

She is the most amazing seed that God has ever sown,
An angel sent from high above, but sadly just to loan.

Simon R Jones

HOME FOR TEA

Climb aboard my magic carpet, share this ride with me.
Let us scale the highest mountains, skim the rolling seas.
Catch a falling star as it quickly passes by,
Higher and higher let us fly upward to the sky.
See the Dome, the Eiffel Tower, the Pyramids and Sphinx,
Notre Dame, Niagara Falls; then stop a while for drinks.
The Leaning Tower of Pisa is next upon my list.
The Coliseum is a must and Venice in the mist.
The windmills they are turning slow along the Zuider Zee.
We're having lots of fun dear friends, I'm glad you came with me!
We'll stretch our legs here for a while and thank the carpet for,
Taking us to realms that we have never seen before.
So jump back on the carpet and hold on tight with me,
Full steam ahead, home we go, we must be back for tea.

Lily Butherway

Rose, Colour Of Spring

When the bells sounded, the dance began
On a morning in a dewy avenue
A line of leaves and dancers mirrored in spring's glass
Far away where the bells fade and the dancers look like leaves
H in rose
Spring's breeze blew her jumper
Rose, the colour of spring.

Stephen Keir

THE LAST STAGE

Today I met a woman
Whom I had not see for years
She cried;
Her heart was dying from
Loneliness,
In a world empty of friends
I gave her a hug
which seemed inappropriate
a mere pittance in lieu of loan.
her tears flowed in abundance,
we talked awhile, there on the street
and went both our own way.
She was old.
Why is being old
a one-way ticket to invisibility?
I remember my great grandmother
she was a funny lady
even to me, a child of five.
She laughed and showed toothless gums
like my little sister, not yet one -
I marvelled
and she talked to me
of things I could not see
and did not know.
She still had time on her hands.

Lila Joseph

The Photo

There was that huge black and white photo
of a famous writer hanging on the wall,
his eyes taken out by sniper bullets

I pushed my index finger
into each hole, perhaps to see
how far one's blind hatred could go

I used to stare at the same portrait,
grainy and shrunk, in my high school
textbook, hoping that I would detect
what it was that made someone
a great writer, a kind of good-natured,
yet canny smile that slightly pudgy cheeks
tried to suppress, two thin tufts
of hair sticking out of the wide-brimmed hat
tilted back, marking a long evening
of lively discussions accompanied by bottles
of some good imported wine, and
the eyes that looked straight at you
with some all-seeing bemused indifference

All the books, including yours, are gone;
get out, they pick up movements in there,
came the raspy voice of the former super,
who shuffled nervously in the corridor
of the publishing house, holding a set of keys,
though all doors had been blown out

But, I just stood there, waiting to be
discovered by a bullet that would erase all
memory, for the mind loses its senses
when it no longer remembers what to forget.

Mario Susko

THUNDER

(A poem for Daniel)

The sky grew dark the wind was strong
birds and animals sensed all was wrong.
A fox ran swiftly to his lair, his vixen quietly waiting there.
Trees bending in the gale scattering leaves asunder
suddenly from the sky a frightening roar of thunder.
Thunder, thunder all around bellowing and roaring - a horrid sound.
The storm grew fierce, lightning flashed
all hope of peace by then was dashed.

An hour went by, or maybe two
what were the birds and animals to do?
Then, without warning, the thunder stopped roaring.
The fox came out and looked around
the world seemed safe no sign of rain
all seemed calm at peace again
and in the distance, so they say,
the thunder gently rolled away.

Madge Sumner

Millennium

(Rev 20 v 1-6)

Stretched out toward the
Infinite. Converging, unforeseen,
An unexpected cusp of past
And future tense. Expanding
To a myriad of possibilities,
Toward a resolution of the counterpoint,
A harmony unfurls - some thousand
Years, maybe, or even more.

Unlike some wind-tossed leaf
That settles to decay,
The autumn of my life
Becoming spring today.

Chris Johnson

SOULMATES

Like two turtle doves entwined
in each other's love.
When you kiss it feels like eternity
has passed.
When in fact it is just only a few
seconds that has elapsed.
Between time and space is your
soulmate.
When you have found each other.
Then you'll know you have found each
other by your feelings for one another.
Then true love can blossom and let no
other stand in the way.
For true love conquers all that stands
in its path.
Through good times and bad
United you'll stand.
This will make you one person
even though you are two individual souls.
For the bonds of love are strong and
will not break.
The everlasting love you two will share.

Tracey Anson

I Love

I love chips and nuggets too,
They're my favourite food in the world for me.
McDonald's is the place that I should be
if my mummy hasn't made any food for me.
I'd dip the chips in the sauce with glee
and my nuggets would come straight over to me,
I'd have some Coke with my favourite tea.
Yes chicken and chips is the food for me.

Jasmeet Sagoo (10)

Red

Did the flames mock you,
While you stoked your hunger for
The red you stole from where?
From everywhere. Cloth,
Plastic, minds, paper.
Did the sparks spit their scorn,
For your eyes as they hinted
Carmine, crimson, scarlet?
Embers glowing a heated
Reminder of who you had become.
Had the fire, conspired its heat,
Its smoke, its anger, turned your
Already molten logic in on you,
Burnt you, scorching the smoulder
Of what remained of you, turning
Again your heart, blood, eyes -
Red?

Mark Thirlwell

DEAREST FEELING

Dearest Feeling, why do you come
When I am feeling down?
Why do you make me feel so desperate
When all I did was frown?
I hate the way you make me despair
And cry all the tears I own.
I have almost lost all I love
Every time that you have shown.
Why do you show such little pity
For I who have carried you far?
And for the ones who have carried us both
- They are the real shining star.
But now I don't want you here,
Forever eating my mind.
Sometimes I will get sad
But not hysterically you'll find.
Please leave and let me be
I've serviced you too much.
I can be sad by myself
Without your frightening touch.
Dearest Feeling, I free you
To go where you may go,
For you Feeling, I feel no more
And never again will you show.

Nykki Welcomme

Forgive Me Not

Let go. Forgive. Forget the bitterness
That buttresses when love is dead:
Most of what's said isn't meant;
Most of what's meant isn't said.

Alan Morrison

To Be Alone

The sun is shining in the sky,
but all alone I'm asking, 'Why?'
It could be day or night outside,
I do not care, in here I hide.

To go outside is such a chore,
my inner self I do explore,
why am I scared when darkness falls,
surrounded by mist and these four walls?

I close my eyes and try to sleep,
but awaken suddenly, and start to weep,
why am I sad with all to live for?
Me to be happy, I ask for no more.

Glyn Norton

Winners And Losers

A man stands shamed,
looking over the sea.
At his lost land.
At his lost love.
At his lost heart.
At his lost friends.

A man stands proud,
looking down from a hill.
At his new land.
At his old love.
At his old courage.
At his old friends.

The men stand dreaming,
looking at what once was.
At what could have been.
At what should have been.
At what they have become.
At what their war has done.

Ben Briggs

VARIETY IS THE SPICE OF LIFE

Hear about love,
talk about love,
sing about love,
work for love.
Variety is the spice of life.

Love God,
love humans,
love animals,
love wealth,
love qualities.
Variety is the spice of life.

Loved yesterday,
love today,
love tomorrow,
love in the morning,
love in the afternoon,
love in the night.
Variety is the spice of life.

Feel love,
taste love,
touch love,
smell love,
think love.
Variety is the spice of life.

Justice Okafor

Dancing In The Moonlight

Into the spotlight of a summer moon the lovers walk
Barefoot, their shadows pooling in the sand
They take the silent stage and as he watches
She turns and smiles, then slowly takes his hand.

In loose embrace and facing one another
Listening for their music from the sea
They sway in rhythm, clasping hands together
He whispers, 'Will you dance with me?'

With shining eyes they focus on each other
Moving now with liquid, lingering grace
And clinging closer, metalled by the moonlight
He bends to kiss her silver face.

She kicks the sand then swiftly changes tempo
They spin apart and whirling limbs untwine
And dance as individual performers
Yet mirror-match each other's steps and line.

He grasps her hand and spins her to him
Then softly strokes her silver ropes of hair
Embracing now their bodies meld together
A fading image in the cooling air.

Sheila Dooley

THE STORM

The sky is black with blows
The storm comes back, stronger
Than ever, raining its blows
Down like hammers furious,
Like this is some virgin attack
Dismembering small things
Lingering within its grasp.

Morning brings a sudden end
A new beginning, a false dawn
The sun never shines more brightly
Than in this bewildering moment of peace
When all storms retreat into nameless
Ionospheres; the eye of a hurricane
Has never seemed this sweet.

He rises from broken ground
And surveys the damage, the bruises
The blood smeared over old scars
Yet he endures, whole within his shell
Knowing that survival has given
Her another moment, another night,
Freedom from the storm.

David Priol

Throwing Stones At The Moon

What then?
Did you find the one you seek?
Did your long journey
take you far,
as far from me you fled?

Are my thoughts
still your thoughts?
Do clouds you see
see me?
When in the darkest night,
as minds unwrap,
do I walk,
as you walk,
in mine?

Do you gaze,
as I gaze.
Knowing that in some far-off place,
am I?
And do
as I do,
in deepest dread,
throwing stones at the moon?

Do you find, as I find,
my thoughts return to you?
Lest the memory unwinds itself
and ties itself anew.

Bob Tose

Tesco's Mayhem

The machine crunches my pound as I grab the trolley,
I pick up a magazine,
I flick the pages through, fast
It sounds like a frilled lizard,
The tins march into the trolley or onto the shelves,
I listen to the 'kerchings' as the till eats the money off people
The trolleys charge back and forth,
While the freezers hum a dull tune
The bread cutter murders the bread,
The breadsticks look tempted to use the slope of cheese as a slide,
As I walk down the aisles
I feel I am being watched,
The food gives you a sorrowful grin as if to say, 'Buy me.'
It is not easy to resist,
I enter the fruit and vegetable section,
The strawberries look sunburnt in the middle,
And the oranges look as orange as the sun.
As I walk past the ice cream it makes my heart turn to ice,
As I come to the end of my shopping trip the mad world dies down.
The trolley is put back,
Ready to charge round again.

Kelly Osborne (11)

UNTITLED

Rain droplets splash to the attic roof
I'm all on my own,
My own little bubble
No need for interference,
All I need is my music
To absorb me into my world, where I
Don't need any reality
As the thunder carries on the
Lightning streaks by, as fast as my memory
Wants to remember -
The times of my past
No need to tell anyone, no need
To get rid of feelings of despair,
Loneliness and depression
All I need is the music, the lyrics
Ringing through my head:
'No need for a damn care' as I start to get into the bath
'No need to carry on, I've nothing to live for,
No will to live with' I submerge myself -
Beneath the water
'Finally, I don't need to carry on,'
No more sound
No nothing.

Katy E Murr

My Other Half Or The Spirit Of Romance

You went from here many long years ago.
But in my mind you still exist, a jewel.
Seventy-two per cent, 'twas said, have made
Contact with partners supposedly deceased.

Your visitations from on high I know
Tell me you are indeed in Heaven bright.
This is a place and state for communion
With our Maker. Where something has been made,
From complex brains to waiting galaxies,
A Maker there must be without a doubt.

This gold, painfully panned from so much dross,
We must keep secure within our truest selves.
Then, like a steering wheel, the brain can bring
The horse power of our heart's desire at last
To Heaven's portal for love's reunion.

Surely this ensures our happy ending!

Desmond Tarrant

Alone In The Meadow

I was solo in the meadow.
Many nights passed by, of pain and anguish
Recrudescing as I meditate upon a cause.
Oh why the fracture in my heart.
A wound that took time to heal.
Letting all be for the supreme justice and
The purity of nature to pronounce rewards.

Just like the way the Earth moves,
Accompanied by the travelling of the sun.
I met her 'Ogirl' my May queen.
A meadowlark always whispering healing
Songs, flying all around me in the meadow.
Perching on the meadow rue and
Chirping at my feet.

What a relief as the fracture healed,
Leaving no scar behind, projected I became
In thoughts and feelings as all around me
Is well, pretty and precious like a gem
Which I always adorn amidst the meadowsweet.

Moses Echeija Okoh

GOODBYE

You,
you make me feel.
Like a coral reef nestled within your ocean.
A black orchid,
amongst the white,
unique,
beautiful,
Precious stone caressing your loving chest.
Treasure of a shipwreck sunk,
many moons ago.
You found me.
I lost you.
The stars no longer tell our story now.
I am numb.
Goodbye.

Emma Flanagan

THE CRYSTAL VASE

A crystal vase in a world of glass
alone stands solemnly on the mantle
Its sparkle gleans shimmers of
light so pure
so to cause shadows to flee far away

In the early morn when the light is dim
or in the even when the whippoorwill calls
patience beckons for the light of day
and the shadows to flee far away

The glass casts shadows long in the night
by the faint glimmer stretched on the wall
they search east for the morning light
and the day which envelops all
to see the vase glisten in the might of day
to stand again in awe

Keith Miller

Dreams

If I laughed so much today . . .
Would you promise to catch my tear
If it fell . . .
If I saw too much, I might just go
Slightly blind,
If I talk too much, you might
Never understand,
If I showed you my way
Do you promise to hold my hand
For eternity . . .
If I told you a secret,
Promise never to forget,
It seems like sun is shining,
In this life of mine,
Even in the best of the
Weathers,
Every day seems like I've . . .
Seen you today for the
First time my mind is asking
Over and over again.
Dreams are never far . . .
Promise to wait for me,
Just a little bit longer
And I say it in a love song.

Kosier Razak

THE MOONLIGHT TALE

On that night,
As the moon was shielded with its halo
And the hamlet was bathed in its brightness,
Drums and songs cheered the night.
The wind listened to our sounds
And flames danced to our songs.
Rosy night snowy orb,
We shall stand to see
The moonlight's kiss on the warm stones.
We shall rise again
To sing once more
The old songs of the great nights
And we shall join our kinsmen
In their treasury of tales
For never will a night be more blissful
Than tonight's tales of yesteryear.

Michael Odega

All By Your Grace

I followed your trail along the
Right lane and
Saw your awesome flame blaze
As I increased my pace
It began to rain
I could not hide my face
Because it was impossible to feign
Though it looked insane
I knew I had lots to gain
As I walked on the rail
I began to pray
I felt pain
But did not wane
Now I feel so great
And I've come to say
Glory be to Your name
It's all by Your grace
That I am here again

Joseph Iregbu

TIME

At light of day
Time - is our deceit, our disbelief,
Our unrequited wish.

Time - is a welcome journey
When we walk its pace
With purity of heart and mind.

When we are stilled and providence grants us
A precious moment of secluded solitude
Where snow-capped peaks
Reveal a dawn of changing hue
And glades hold in their palms
The tranquil, early morning mist,
Time - does not intrude.

World weary travellers
In search of sanctuary or saintly love
May find a momentary, timeless peace.

Before the outside world reveals itself
In such unwelcome haste,
Time - will lie within its narrow, frightening bounds.

Time - allows a short reprieve
When all may journey through those chartered paths.

For those who hear that loving cry
Time - is eternal.

Michael Davidson

Eyes

Drawn in deep,
I'm powerful to resist.
Your passion bathes me.
My senses are heightened,
My skin tingling.
Dragged deeper into the vortex.
I can see your emotions churning,
And your hidden thoughts unleashed,
I can see your naked soul
In your open eyes.

Colette Horsburgh

Uncle Joseph

Why did you have to be taken away so soon it is sad,
You were still young it makes me mad.
With your glowing smile and your cheeky laugh,
You always were cheerful and you liked to act daft.
But that was you Uncle Joseph always thinking of others,
Even though you were the youngest,
You still looked out for your brothers.
That is the person you were,
Always smiling and joking.
You glowed and you were so good-looking,
With your dark hair and eyes of blue,
When I was a child I always looked up to you.
Even when you knew you were dying,
You still made me laugh,
I remember being so upset and start crying,
I never did cry in front of you,
I had a word with my dad, and we both felt so upset and blue
Because you were still a proud man, even near the end,
I am so glad you were my uncle and someone,
I could call a friend.

Christine Denise, Joseph, George Phillips

Aunty

I can touch the crosses
Feel the cold blessed ground
Fall against the tombstone
Weep upon the mound

What were you thinking
Before you made your end?
Then you took that final step
Your mind to try and mend

Features blurred together
Decaying over time
Sickness eating from within
Your face so close to mine

Father cracking from within
Desperate to hide the hole
Daddy, don't be strong for me
Please heal your broken soul

Will you be there waiting
In gowns of flowing white?
Is your sin forgiven?
Are you standing in the light?

I will keep on walking
Down this winding road
Steps I'll keep on taking
Despite the heavy load

Kathleen Westcott

THE SUNDIAL

Its shadow always shrinking
Or enlarging as time progresses,

Its reliance in the sun
Is one thing it never confesses,

Each day it loyally stands alone -
An imposer to passers-by

And because some think it ugly,
Time's a solace it always supplies.

Sarah Braithwaite

A TRIBUTE TO SADIE, A WONDERFUL DOG

(1986-1999)

Though Sadie is not with us, or near at hand to see
She will always be in our hearts, and thought of lovingly,
Fond of family and people, special times we can recall
As Sadie was so special and liked by one and all.

Always pleased to see you much affection she would make
And gladly eat the titbits, like biscuits, sweets or cake,
Underneath the kitchen table was the place she liked to be
Never far from people, who called in for chats and tea.

In our caring, loving home for 13 years, to live was meant
With happy, treasured memories of life spent quite content,
The house now seems so empty, it's hard to comprehend
Much more than a dog to us, she was a faithful friend.

Now her time with us is over, no more walks to take,
She will never be forgotten and worth every tear we make.
Everyone will miss her, Sadie was one of nature's best,
Now resides here in the garden, where forever she can rest.

Geraldine S Stephenson

ANNE FRANK

(Kingston University Exhibition, Summer '98)

It makes me weep when I see
man's wicked inhumanity.
That young girl who should be free
was facing her immortality.
And all that is truth and all that is good
should give our wicked hearts a prod.
Such scenes scorch the memory
of man's immorality.

Athena

BEE

I don't know whether
That bee
Squirming on the ground
Was disabled
Or trying to scratch its back.
I would like to have helped it, but

Splat!

A child had spied
The cute fluttering creature,
Waddled up to it,
Crushed it with an eager foot,
Proclaimed, 'It got died.'

So when I see a bee
I think of my faith in humanity.
Sometimes its wings are illuminated by the sun,
At others it struggles.

Neil Laurenson

WHAT IS THE . . . OCEAN?

The ocean, is a place for fun,
that will take you away on a magical journey.

It has a mind of its own,
like a raging bull out of control.

Sometimes it is calm,
with the waves lapping on the golden sands.

The ocean, is a giant home to many underwater creatures,
that depend on it to give them shelter.

In storms, it is like a hurricane
wanting to destroy every boat in sight.

Emily May Williams (11)

What Is The . . . Ocean?

(Original poem by Emily May Williams, aged 11 years.
Revised and enlarged by Edward James Williams 18/8/2004)

The ocean, is a place for fun,
enjoyed by each and everyone,
It can take you far away,
for maybe a month or only a day,
On a magical seaborne journey.

It has a mind of its very own,
and round the world inclines to roam,
At times it's like a raging bull,
depending on the tidal pull,
When it runs out of control.

Sometimes it is calm,
when wind and waves subside,
With the scent of the briny balm,
washing in on the flowing tide,
Lapping on the golden sands.

The ocean, is a giant home,
where underwater creatures hide,
Depending on its surging foam,
and wind-blown currents deftly ride,
To give a watery shelter.

In storms, it is like a hurricane,
with gusting winds and slanting rain,
It seems to want all craft to drown,
the undercurrents to pull them down,
To destroy every boat in sight.

Then the ocean will calm become,
kind fate will rescue everyone,
Once more they sail and learn to cope,
and with The Saviour live in hope,
As the ocean flows unceasingly.

Edward James Williams (A Bystander Poet)

The Child In The Graveyard

The child and his bottle of water full
Awaits the visitor's generous handful.
The child greets the visitor good morn
With his face of wrinkles like weeds borne
By the waves of time hollowed in the ground.
In his dormant eyes lies a solitary cloud
That sunshine neglects to clear away,
And homely warmth to it finds no way.
His rags show his bones unclothed.
His bare feet chopped and furrowed
Bear kinship with the dried brown soil.
It is in this graveyard he is left to toil.
To gain a visitor's mercy is a matter of luck
Among other children who from the graves they suck
Their daily bread and reckon themselves full.
The child waters the newly-grown ivy,
Then sweeps with his hands the cemented grave,
And takes a coin and bows his thankful face,
And once again, he goes to queue in his eternal place.

Hayat Diyen

Smuggler's Cove

The silver moon
Shining on a velvet sea
As a boat, slowly draws to shore
And as it is beached
From out of the shadows
A group of men quickly appear
To help unload the cargo of contraband
Of brandies and wines, for gentlemen,
Silks and fine laces for ladies
Into the cave mouth they go
To a narrow passage
Leading to a larger opening
Like an Aladdin's cave
There the goods are stored, till needed
But hurry they must
As revenue men are on their trail
Moving into the shadows
They quickly disappear
To outwit the King's men, once more.

Alice Higham

Hobbies

The morning chores have come and gone,
Everything's ready to eat.
It's nice to sit down and dream in the sun,
It's a chance to put up my feet.

Now, my husband has started to make his own wine,
As a hobby, it keeps him quite busy -
But he seems to be at it for most of the time,
And sometimes it makes him quite dizzy.

At present I'm watching two jars in the sun,
One red and one white on the bubble,
It's really relaxing to see how it's done,
It's the tasting that causes the trouble!

'Pop' goes the wine through the jar and the tube,
Over and over again.
Like a lullaby, it's a soft interlude,
Like the sound of the falling rain.

I'll just have a drop of the Plum '91,
Or Orange and Pear '92,
The Cowslip 1990, I'd recommend too,
Will you have a little one?
Those jars in the sun; are there three there
Or one on the bubble?

The elderflower wine, it tastes quite divine,
I *am* in a bit of a muddle.
I don't know what you think,
You know I don't drink -
It's the *tasting* that causes the trouble!

Kay Liepins

FLOODING

The rain is unceasing
No watch party is seen
By the local authorities
After the flooding that's been

The river banks tremble
Until at last they subside
Scattering their debris
Over green countryside

Houses are flooded
Catching tenants asleep
They awake to this horror
And they only can weep

Some have taken out insurance
Others have left this to fate
And so they've lost everything
Which is sad to relate

It is time local councils
Built up river banks
As all that they're doing
Is to keep firing blanks.

Lachlan Taylor

The World Is A Bus

Disgusted, abused and bitterly cold
I can't seem to embrace the new and get rid of the old
Deciding to live on a one-man island
Isn't all it's cracked up to be
Walking around lost in a trance
Impenetrable to a word or a glance

To me the world is a bus
People get on and off, some make a fuss
It's no point me getting attached
When you could be getting off at the next stop
But there was a little girl sitting next to me one day
She started singing a song about flapping wings and flying away

On the bottom deck, she was the smallest person there
She had the smallest voice but everyone turned to stare
She sang out of tune but her voice sounded so soothing
Because it had been untouched by the harsh reality of the world
I wondered if I could be a little girl again that way
What I would sing or what I would say

I would enquire about you, like a child when you sat next to me
And if we got on really well, I might even sit on your knee
I would still feel sad, when you got off at your stop
But I would wave you goodbye and hope we meet again
As we grow, we change our voices so they fit with the key
But even though the little girl was out of tune, everyone on the bus was in harmony

Sita Dinanauth

Hannah I Love You

Hannah, I love you, every day . . .
more than words can say,
when you were born
(you made me very happy, when you yawn!)
until I can, will love you forever,
so always, be very clever!

I hope you will always be kind and nice,
and never do any illegal vice(s)!
Do well at school
and never be a silly fool!

You like watching 'Grease'
and playing with your niece(s)!
Dido, Britney and Busted
you like, as you listen to their music, lying in bed.

Go with your heart,
if you are not happy with it, don't take part,
ie, no 'cigs', crime or drugs,
otherwise you end up like a 'silly mug'!

Never do anything to others in spite,
that you wouldn't, yourself like!

Barry Ryan

TALKING TO VOICES WITHIN

Bumblebee on the tree tell me what you want
A bucket full of rainbow dust
A fallen star from the sky above

I aim to please
I aim to be
Will you help me to become?

As a drop of water slowly caresses my face
A symbol of sorrow travelling down my cheek
My only wish is to be complete

You are my centre
My everything
Will you help me to become?

Nothingness threatens to envelop my world of dreams
Answers are needed but cannot be found
Will you not give me the recipe to succeed?

Angel in the tree
Can you not see
Will you help me to become?

Filip Aggestam

Death And Life

In death there is life
In life there is death
The twin that is inseparable
Together they come
Together they work

At birth life begins
At birth death begins
Everyday life creates
Everyday death destroys
In harmony they move
A smooth rhythmic flow

The celebration of life
Is done in death
The preparation for death
Begins in life
A paradox
A never-ending cycle

He who wants to live
Must first die
And he who wants to die
Must be alive
A transition
We are yet to understand

In life there is death
In death there is life
The preparation for both
Starts before life
And continues after death

Oriyomi A Lawal

LOOKING BACK

When we close our eyes we can see the smiles
On the young faces that were our youth
We know that when we let go and open them up
We might be discouraged by the truth

When we smell the fresh rain on the hot road
It reminds us of the many friends we had
We promised that we would never grow old
And yet our current situation makes us sad

When we were looking at the clouds of dreams
Floating us a beautiful lie to be set free
We felt that our future was set in stone
But I guess some things weren't meant to be

We love this life, don't get us wrong
It has always treated us so right
But as you know everyone needs to let go
Before the pressure starts to bite

David Krupa

WRITTEN IN STONE

Great walls of might,
Stand tall and stand proud.
Though crumbling slightly,
Speak their word loud.

Stones - cold and rough,
Built up so high.
Though aging's their surface
The history won't die.

For old it may be,
But strong it is too.
Still bold throughout ages,
Of me and of you.

In glory 'tis bathed,
And in splendour 'tis crowned.
So much history it tells,
Yet so much to be found.

Though 'tis only ruins,
Those ruins do hold
The past of our country,
Victorious and old.

Victoria Morley

The Truth

Incandescent with white-hot rage,
I lie here in my furious grave.

You think I am gone.
Safely locked in my box.
My eyes won't see. My ears won't hear.

You think you are free to spin your tales of fate,
to spin our lives into a web
of lies that catch our souls like flies.

But I was there, darling,
when you wrote those letters.
I stood behind you and watched
your pen leak excuses, ink made from our blood.
Weaving your pages of myths.

I, your first wife. I inevitably died.
Mad thing that I was.
How else could it end?

Like a puppet I jerked into hatred of her.
But now I have seen. Now I have heard.
I wrote the rival. You wrote the other.
Now the unlikely partnership forms
and we, we write the truth.

Look over your shoulder, dear, at all times.
Keep a watch in every mirror you see.
Be afraid every time that the telephone rings.
Listen out for unexpected knocks at the door.

One of these days, my love, one of these days.

We *will* rise from the ashes. We will have our revenge.
We will write the final chapter of this myth.
Two suicides will drag this god to his death.

One of these days, my love, one of these days.

Morney Wilson

LIZARD DAY

Quick-eyed lizard under lazy rock
quite still, no twitch or flicker
in suspended animation
until a muscle moves
it ventures out to test the scornful sun
which, like a hot blanket, wraps itself round human heads
in just a moment
whose burning eye still drives this chiselled land
of greens and greys, of quiver trees
of those that know to send their roots
down, down beneath its arid mantle.

Lizard darts across the path
retreats again and scurries into shade
the angry glare there hard upon its tail;
nearby the dassie, busy, nose probing sandy soil
its furry coat designed
for burrowing as for basking;
meanwhile, as dusk draws on, cicadas sing
the distant trees dissolve in darkness
maybe giraffe will forage, springbok make their way
and dreams may dance among the stars
one night in Africa.

Michael Brueck

Dazzling

Stimulation arouses my mind
I see you only as compassionate and kind,
Love bedazzles my emotions
Engaging my spirit as an ocean.

I promise to spend my love on you
This promise I give to Andy is true
Darling and dear are not enough
My love is not rough.

No, it's smooth, serene and suave
Without you my darling I starve
My emotions feed upon your gaze
It sets my heart ablaze.

Denise Shaw

The White Horse

By removing turf men found,
Many years ago,
They could reveal the chalk
Hidden down below.
Carefully they made a horse
Which can be seen there still,
It is always known of course,
As the white horse on the hill.
In a field further down
A white horse grazes,
Unaware of the horse of chalk
As it eats the grass and daisies.
Yet the chalk horse up above,
Made long ago with love,
Forms a backdrop for us to see
A legend from our history.

Margaret Nixon

TWO NICE LADIES

Having broken my right ankle in two places
I went for massage in the local physiotherapy salon
Where everything was new and up to date
And the smiles always made me feel welcome

Much pleasure and healing I got in this salon
Two beautiful ladies with God's healing power
My legs became spritely like a bird on the hop
My spirits much lighter and never flopped

I am now an old woman who walks with a stick
But my legs are much stronger and don't go stiff
I now walk much further and feel very fit
So thank you God, Kay and Marie

I sometimes see them when I'm out
I get a smile and a kiss on my cheek
They look happy as they talk to me
Seeing these ladies is my treat

We remember each other with a card every Christmas
These two ladies I'll never forget
Kay and Marie are the good examples
For the good, clean Britain which is yet to be

Hetty Foster

WALKING ALONE

It would be nice if someone said hello,
Pass the time of day and ask how things go
To say how well you look, to boost your ego
And admire your step, it seems lighter, you know.

Living alone is not all it could be
From one week to the next, the days flee
Time won't stand still for pensioners like me
But thank God I can talk, walk, hear, and see.

Some folk are kind and offer a hand
Young teenagers offer their seat, and stand
So nice to have someone open a door once more
And help across the road is a blessing for sure.

But feeling the loss of one's partner and friends
And wishing that old time memories never end
Being so grateful, and with head held high
There's always another day, to welcome a passer-by.

C King

ANGLING

Not just by chance
You'd cast your glance,
Until your eye met mine.

That baited look
Soon had me hooked.
The first bite on your line.

Then with a grin
You reeled me in
Without an inch of slack.

But not a patch
On last night's catch
You coolly tossed me back.

Chris Scriven

SHOUT

If you feel you have nowhere to turn,
And you're hurting deep inside,
Find the strength within you.
Be brave and confide.
Talk to someone you can trust,
And try not to feel bad,
Because *you're important,*
You've done no wrong.
And shouldn't feel sad.
Once you've found a person that listens,
The relief for you is immense.
Just *talking* and being *listened* to,
Really does make sense.
So don't bottle anything up.
Find the courage to speak out.
Tell yourself, *'I am important.'*
Don't whisper, *shout.*
You will be listened to,
And help is there for you.
Please don't suffer alone,
Unleash your fears and start anew.

Anne Leeson

ACCESS LAW

The end of the year, what a relief to us
It's being enjoyable as it's fun and work
And makes you think and learn and making
You prepared for university as Jo, our Access
Teacher is our friend and a star who never
Stops helping us and sharing our work
She is funny and witty, she has long hair
Which makes her look ten times tall
And she loves that as she can look at us
And say what she wants to say.
I recommend Access Law to anyone who
Wants to do it as it gives you skills to
Face the world and gain confidence
To write and talk and feel nice
That you have established something
Yourself as our teacher Jo knows how
She has a big brain and quick in her
Lessons and good time-keeper that makes
Her rare and the best to have, hope to see
You next year as no one does it better than you
As it would not be the same, you are our star, so keep
It up and keep on smiling as you are special.
Thank you for all your help on behalf of my class as well.

F Jackson

Feared Am I

I don't have any preference between rich or the poor
Age doesn't come into it, neither the race, nor the creed
My presence, my reason, my only aim
Is to bring sickness, sadness and cause oh so much pain
Not counting on the grief and the anguish of those I leave behind
No mercy have I as tears fall in vain
Along with each and every victim that I may claim
Every individual is fearful of I
But then I'm not known as the big I, you know me as the big C.

Susan Barker

LILY

Over the years we've loved tending our flowers.
In the garden we have spent hours and hours.

They've always filled us with such awe
And it's never been, to us, a chore.

With their marvellous scent and glorious colour,
We could never decide which ones we most favour.

Well, not until now, we have a gorgeous Lily.
She has Grandad and I acting rather silly.

With a golden crown and dancing eyes
She shoos away bees and chases butterflies.

For the past few years she's also spent hours
Romping madly among our beautiful flowers.

But none of them are quite so fair
As our lovely Lily with the golden hair.

K Moran

Walk With Me Home

Jesus our Saviour had to suffer and die,
For our sins he perished at far Calvary.
All the power of Heaven on the Earth down below,
Yet, to the cruel cross He was willing to go.

So pure, unblemished, not a sin on His soul,
But for our transgressions He surrendered His all.
Tested by Satan's temptations, and fasting.
He died that we might have life everlasting.

Again o'er the world He is silently sighing,
So many of His children in sin still are dying.
How sadly we reject Him and murder each other,
We still cannot see every man is a brother!

How long will we turn from His blessed teaching,
As so often He stood in the temple court preaching,
Reading the scriptures, and healing the maimed,
All that forgotten? We should feel so ashamed.

In meekness but with gladness, let's take His hand,
With sadness let's feel the wound in his palm.
Let Him lead us with joy, along that pathway well known,
And hear Him gently whisper, 'Walk with Me home.'

Isaac Smith

A SUNNIER MOOD

There's a sunnier mood
Now autumn is here
I'm not a misery
But filled
With good cheer
Yes, a sunnier mood
Now summer has gone
Perhaps it's
Mental illness
I wish
Was foregone.

Philip Allen

Fourfeit!

It was weekend in the convent
The nuns were getting bored
They decided to try a crossword
Which most of them enjoyed
Time had been passing slowly
With little there to do
It was alright being 'holy'
But that stunted points of view
Their superior did then enter
And asked to join the fun
She speedily found the answers
All except the final one
She thought about it quickly
'Would you here accept a bet?
A day off if any of you can beat me
And that last word you can get!
There are only left four letters
Two blank spaces, then *IT*
Found well below a budgie's lettuce.'
She yelled, 'That is a day off for *me!*'
She grinned at all the 'players'
Who had had their answers hidden
Then she blushed and said some prayers
Then erased what she had written!

Yes - she *had* found the answer hidden
And it did certainly fit
But I'm afraid such words are forbidden
The answer - instead - was *grit!*

Jon El Wright

Dead Dreams

Going home, on a bus,
I saw your face.
Just a glimpse
In the throng
Of the great rat race.

On a train
Through the window,
As it thundered by,
Misty and unclear
In the pouring rain.

In a car
As it passed,
When you turned your head,
Then the smile
And the illusion fled.

I still look!
Maybe one day
It will be you.
When we meet
What will I say?

Or maybe you
Will wave!
Just passing by,
Greeting me as a friend,
And I will be brave.

But the tears I'll shed
When you've passed by,
You will never see.
For what we had
Is long since dead!

Joan May Wills

INSPIRATION

I'm now in my thirties,
Two growing-up teens,
Wondering where the years have gone?
Once living beyond my means,
I took people and things for granted when young,
Now sorry for the mistakes I've once done.
Losing my wonderful inspiration,
My dear sweet mum,
But knowing her pain-free journey has now begun,
Then meeting my new man –
Trevor makes me feel safe and new,
Having my faith, man, daughters -
My new life's so true.
So don't give up when life gets tough,
Brush yourself down when people get rough,
Believe in your faith and those you love,
Be an example of a Christian
And to those we've lost above.
Sometimes we lose someone we can never replace,
No one will come close - not even a trace.
But take with you one of their wonderful ways,
And they'll live on inside you,
Smiling for you on sad days.

Nina Bates

The Weight Of Thunder

The eyelids twitch
Reflections in gemstones
Majestic love a virtual hologram
Such a Godsend
And a blessing for the poor man in hand-me-downs.
A temporary burning sensation
Wakes him from his slumber
The hourglass is shattered
And the sand recycled.
A walk on the beach
A stained-glass window.
Shimmering miracles bathe his weathered features.
An old man finding shelter
In a crumbling village church.
Sermons and evensong a memory
Loyal dog between the pews.
A breeze turns Matthew into Mark
Troubled dreams of possible outcomes
Linger in the memory.
An unmarked grave
A life of rain.
Eyelids feel the weight of thunder
And a cleansing takes place.
The shepherd struggles to penetrate
And a royal love returns.
Diamonds sparkle in the soul
The heart falters
And the wandering is over.

John Hobbs

CAPTIVE

When it hurts so much you just want to cry,
From the tips of your toes right up to the sky.
To watch the pain in someone's eyes,
As they are pushed around, terrorised.
Left with no food and with nothing to drink,
It is hard to imagine what these people think.
Their hopes are shattered, lifetimes gone,
As they are all blown up by one single bomb.

Emily Clark (13)

My Love For You

My love for you
Feels good, feels right
I long to hold you
Through the night

When we touch
When we kiss
How can anything
Feel better than this?

Now it's ended
I will endeavour
My love for you
Will last forever.

David Normington

STAR-BRIGHT

Starlit nights
Mist asunder
Peace of night
No sound of thunder

Gazing at the points of light
Amazing man, shining so bright
Vastness in the space complete
Infinite, my eyes to meet.

Troubles lessen in intensity,
To minimise is the propensity
Of these stars defying description
Everlasting, need no inscription.

In proportion is man's struggle,
Mastered, straightened, no reason to juggle,
Taken with the eternal sameness
Heals the emotions, cures the lameness.

Puts the mind on the right track
No more bothered with 'alas alack',
Senses by this sight becalmed
Troubles vanished - by nothing harmed.

Soothed, gentled, no feelings ruffled
Blest by the daylight, the stars now muffled
By the sun, our closest star
From furthest points must seem afar.

William C E Howe

THE GHOST TRAIN

a journey to the house of the elders
haunted with the dust of memories
the forgotten village without a road
where monkeys form a travesty

the Hong Kong Island tram
a sudden lurch of erratic movement
like the ghost train on English pier
the joy and sadness of a fading summer

across the futuristic city
faces ever watchful
collude the silent past abandoned

as I the lonely figure on the tram
become the object of their scrutiny

and now the path I walk
takes me past the shuttered window
to hear again that sound
through banana and bamboo grove
the pain of the woman who cried in the night

Guy Arnold

LIFE COLOURS

A picture is painted on the canvas of life,
colours are varied, emotions rife,
sometimes bright colours are the hue,
but pictures are often tinged with blue,
black and grey dull scenes portray,
life is filled with dismay,
some days are painted with a pretty mauve,
others in colours that we loathe,
only the Lord knows why this variety is needed,
and His teachings must be heeded.

N Roskilly

Opportunity Knocked

Slumbering, lumbering
Getting on by
Dragging my feet
But the question is why
How did I land in this misery
This torment
This time waste
Eight-hour drudgery
If clocks could be wound back
My hours would be spent
Studying, learning
About what the facts meant
The biggest mistake
And my largest crime
Is missing my chances
And wasting my time.

Mark Guy

Beslan

O' Beslan
O' Beslan

How can such evil fester
in the human heart?

The tears of the world
will flow forever.

Jessica Boak

TERROR

Is all hope lost? Is this who we are,
Shadows, echoes of our true design?

The tower crumbled to the ground.
Shock, muted screams, echoed around the world.
Dust. Rubble. Empty hearts numb with loss, stunned . . .

Unchecked. Tears fill my eyes, we, so far from Eden.
Facts unfold before me. My heart dissolved.
Time slows. Faces, tearstained and dusted with grief.

We are our own nightmares.
These guilty men. A dark collection of hate.
So misguided, forgotten, hate consuming them.

Were they not babes too in the arms of loving mothers?
Once as pure as an empty canvas.

Look upon the children in your own arms, in your own lives
Love harder, guide wisely. Let them hear the stories.

Help them to find once more, Eden.
Hope is not lost. It is reflected in the eyes of our children.

Shirley Cawte

Fewer Rooms

Old books, tie-dies, some prints the leaves chalk-rubbed.
Live match, a spark, a blaze, the fire, the tears.
And forty years of children's toil and sweat
And pungent memories never to forget
Drifting in smoke to territories unknown.
And why? Because there is no longer room
To hoard those tear-torn treasures from the past.
The move, the move, the move, is all I hear.
No stairs, no stars less work and fewer rooms
To tend and clean and care for. What a bore!
Words slithering like vipers to my ear.
Papers, tie-dies and books, now blackened crisps
Moving like midges in the morning sun,
The smoky ghost-like shadows of the spoil
Put voice and faces to the writhing wisps
'Please Miss,' she lisps, 'I'm trying to understand
What B and C and X can really be.'
The drip-drop sweat paints patterns pink and black.
'But B is known and C you must find out.
Just think Belinda. Think to find what X can be.'
The X the X the X is the unknown.
Exit my treasures. Flash floods will not restore.
We move to the unloved, unlived, unknown , un-memoried new abode.

Mary Froggett

View From A Nudist Beach

You've got big feet,
And I never knew it, till you took your clothes off.
Then all of a sudden, there they were,
My eyes fixed to them like glue.
You who had been forever clothed in cotton.
I had forgotten that you would be
Someone different with not a lot on.

Jon Poole

A Child's-Eye View

I kissed the kitten and it kissed me
I stroked the puppy and it licked me
ain't it funny what you can do when you are only three
like stand in the middle of a town
and against a wall or standing tree
unzip and have a pee

look in shop windows
your nose pressed near flat against its glass
drooling over its jars full of candy
cuddle up to your sister just to pull her curls
walk all the way home, backwards
missing the cracks in the pavements but not the puddles

kick a football into a tree
have Daddy climb up to see
if that above is a bird's nest or not
funny what people do for you
when you are but a kid of three
for in an instant they will drop to their hands and knees

just to get down to your level
no need to, thinks me
for I would rather be riding up high
sat on Dad's broad shoulders and view
the world and the garden next door
where, when I'm bored my ball is thrown.

Maurice Hope

THE FARMER'S BOY

When he was a little boy, he didn't want to be
A pilot or a sailor, and sail away to sea
He didn't want to be a soldier, a weapon in his hand
But to live in the country, and help the farmer with his land
He didn't want to be a doctor, he was quite a clever boy
And had he become one, he'd be his mother's pride and joy
He said he'd move to Cornwall to reap and plough the land
He wanted to be a farmer's boy, that's what he had planned
He didn't want to be a train driver and drive the Flying Scot
Or be a judge or a lawyer, no, he certainly did not!

He wanted to milk the cows and feed the porkers too
And help with the hens, that's what he'd like to do

And early in the spring, sometimes chilly winds would blow
He'd help to deliver calves, and wheat and barley sow.

On market day they'd get up early and to the market go
That farmer taught him everything he felt the boy should know
And when my farmer's boy has grown, we'll just have to wait and see
He'll own a large farm of his own and a master farmer be.

P Williams

My Obsession

I love to see things spick and span
From puffing up cushions to that dirty pan
I seem to get enjoyment in the things I clean
My place is like a palace, all my surfaces have a sheen

I start downstairs in the kitchen maybe
Then I do all the first floor before my cup of tea
After my break I head upstairs
I think I will tackle the bathroom, that seems the worst

Washing, dusting, scrubbing the floors
Making beds, ironing and polishing the brass on the doors
The work is not hard, I do it with ease
But with the dust I disturb, it makes me sneeze.

Then I look back with a smile on my face
Everything perfect not a thing out of place
I get job satisfaction with all the work that I do
I love to see a clean home
'Don't you?'

Barbara Jackson

My Child

Your first breath, your first cry
My heart leapt with joy
My life has new meaning and now I know why
I've waited for this moment and now that you're here
My reason for living has become clear
I cannot comprehend that I gave you life
But I promise to protect you with all of my might
My sweet child, my blessing, I'm so overwhelmed
The missing link in my life I have finally found
I now understand why you are here with me
You were meant to be mine, my destiny
As I look into your eyes, I see perfection so new
I never imagined I could have this feeling so true
I feel love, joy, thanks and elation and awe
I love you now and forever more
My life is fulfilled, I now understand
The magic of God's creation in my hands

Korena Marie Baker

Freedom

Oh to be a bird on a windy day!
Gliding and soaring every which way
Landing on branches
Swaying to and fro
Making your mind up
Which way to go.

Freedom!

Jack Adam

Why Love?

Why is it when we meet my heart races so fast?
When we are together the time doesn't seem to last?
Why do the moments apart seem longer every time?
And the biggest why, why are you mine?

I cannot believe that I have done something so grand
To have you want me, is something I don't really understand
But I won't try and question it too hard
Just in case I find it's all a façade

Instead I will just sit and thank my lucky stars
I don't need lots of money or fancy cars
All I need is what you give to me
Your tender love for all the world to see.

William Wilkinson

Signs Of Life

Signs of love are hearts and flowers,
Signs of time are minutes and hours,
Signs of life are babies crying,
Signs of death are people dying.

From birth we grow and map our lives,
Through teenage years, then husbands and wives,
In middle age, we think we've won,
But then we're old and it's over and done.

We could be happy, we could be sad,
We could be angry, alone or mad,
We could give up, before we start,
We could die young of a broken heart.

The choice is ours yes, me and you,
Whatever we choose, whatever we do,
So smile at all the things around,
You'll be surprised at what you've found.

Samantha Walsh

Satan And Eve

(The Tempter never had a chance)

He crouched in the clothing bushes,
Watched her like a desert man
Watches rain clouds scud and loll,
She was the last created thing,
The pinnacle.
Created from a milky, smooth rib.
Soft and curved and . . .
No, the eyes. The eyes were the things to watch,
The things to wish for.
Electric-green.
The smile. A crescent joy.
In that slip of time the adversary,
Would have cast his pride like lead,
And gone to her and buried deep his head,
In the heaven of her hair,
Laid his hand deep,
Kissed her lips with fingertips.
Better to serve in love than rule in Hell.
But then his eyes saw the man.
This, he thought to her, this you would love?
This bobbing ape, this puppetry,
Of skin and fluids base.
This stinking, drinking thing.
Him, you love well?
For this you'd scorn the love of King of Hell?
For she was in his arms now,
And the sighs, the eye-smiles and the subtle tone of love,
Were comets to the once bright angel's eyes,
That seared the draggling goodness in his breast
Lucifer died, for good and all, in a mulberry bush.
Only Satan lived to tell the tale.
'You'll burn,' he whispered to her.
I'll see you burn.

Neil K Sharpson

The Eye Of The Beholder

Strange how we see beauty
It's true what they say
It's in the eye of the beholder
For God made us that way
A man who's bent and wizened
Has a beautiful young wife
And the way she attends to all his needs
Shows she's given him her life
A child who cannot lift his head
Is dribbling down his chin
Has a beauty known just to his mum
For she just cares for him
It's a good job we don't all see beauty
The same as our fellow man
For the beauty inside is the beauty that counts
We must hold onto that if we can.

Grace Divine

UNTITLED

Sometimes I feel your pain
Kills me slowly
That I have lost you

Crawled circles
To love you

To know that death has befriended you
Jealousy is aroused within me

That he's smouldered your body
Your soul buried in a thousand worlds

And I dance
Without moving in my own.

Teresa Morgan

Red Like Wine

Touches my lips
Liquid fire
Fuel in my veins
Electric rain
Bread broken
Divine meal
Flesh living
Peace be still
Intoxicating
Spirit rising
Holy grapevine
Bittersweet
Red like wine.

Emma Akuffo

Where Were You?

They sat in their hundreds
Cramped on the floor
Men, women and children
Where were you?
Their hands on their heads
Terrified
Where were you?

Their captors paraded around
Armed with guns, knives and bombs
Where were you?

They were frightened and scared
Where were you?

They begged and pleaded
Where were you?

They were hungry and thirsty
Where were you?

They ran and screamed for help
As bullets rained down on them
Like a violent thunderstorm
Where were you?

Finally the death toll
So many lives taken
Why?
Where were you, God?
Where were you?

Pauline E Reynolds

Hell At Heights

The witches fly high at night,
On their supersonic brooms.
Screaming and yelling abuse,
Happiness I presume!

Blind of their ugliness within,
They have nothing of their own.
Filled with jealousy and greed,
Descent people leave well alone!

Behind the moving clouds,
The moon hides in shame.
Until their hysteria subsides,
Life will never be the same.

Animals seek retreat,
From the ghostly atmosphere.
Spooky frightening feelings,
Knowing their presence is near!

Then the evil sort of silence,
Calm and tranquillity looms.
For once again the moon appears,
As peace on Earth presumes!

Ann Beard

LONE WOLF

Lone wolf, shy, reserved,
Hiding through the day,
Pondering deepest thoughts,
Growling to keep people away.

Rarely letting anyone close,
Fearing your sharp claws,
Bounding through the undergrowth,
Hiding your perceived flaws,

No one knows the real you,
Lonely, hurting inside,
Trying to find your way in life,
To survive fate's rough ride,

You hide yourself in dark shadows,
And under a blackening sky,
Why is it you allow so few close,
Are you worried you may cry?

Only a couple can see through,
Your lone wolf disguise,
But a single smile or happy word,
And you're open to their eyes,

You're not as bad as you think,
People like you too,
You can be great if only you try,
To see things as they do,

People will love you for who you are,
Not for this wolf, alone,
Release the human inside of you,
Stop trying to be unknown.

Mitch Cokien

The Mirror Never Lies

Mirror, mirror on the wall
Why can't you make me slim and tall?
Instead of the image you always portray
I'm sure I wasn't built this way!

You could show some tact, be a little discreet
Add a little distance from my head to my feet!
It would be appreciated - would make me less grumpy
I don't like to see - small, fat and dumpy!

What's that you say? Now just be quiet!
Just work some magic, don't mention 'diet'!
I mean what I say and I say what I mean
Just make me willowy, tall and lean

Yes, I'm asking too much, I hear what you say
Mission impossible - OK! OK!
I'll ask no more, I'll accept what I see
And try to be happy with fat frumpy me!

Cathy Robertson

Ruth-Emmie

Alone I sit upon my bed,
watching the planes go by!
The imaginations that fill my head,
most of my truth has been a lie!

It starts to rain now, *ssshh,*
my window mists up with fog!
A lonely cat creeps under a car,
I gather it has more sense than my dog!

Knock, knock, knock, I hear on my door,
my father, he comes to light.
'We're off to Milton Keynes, my dear,'
adventurous I am, could be in for a fright.

A business meeting, how boring how old,
I should have stayed at home.
A lad I hear, Tyrone, I'm told,
that's sure to change my tune!

A back door we seek,
to escape the boredom
Steamy, frisky, passion!
My dreams come true,
I'll cling to you
As if a piece of fashion!

It's not what I expected, no
it actually turned out well.
We're meeting up in two weeks' time,
but what happens I will not tell!

Joseph Larkin

Frigid Waters

Riverboat edging
towards the shore,
water bursting
through the floor.

Captain shouting
'Throttle at full thrust!'
current pulling,
as boards
creek and toss.

Darkness falls,
river moves to sea;
it's the frigid waters
that keep us
beneath.

James Scott

The Strength Inside You

You can't go from bad to worse,
Think about the past,
The good times and the fun we had,
I'm sure it's in there somewhere,
Why do you neglect it so?
Surely it's unfair,
Does the past mean more to me than you?
Do you have to follow in your father's footsteps?
Questions that remain unanswered,
In a world of opportunity,
Rise to the challenge,
Make your goals,
I respect you more than you will know,
Too many people have taken your route,
And I know your potential,
So stand up and fight,
Forget your past,
For the future isn't far away,
And I know you can do it,
The strength is inside you.

Chris Campbell

All Your Days

We wake up each morning
Gladly greet our new day
Will this be a hard one?
Only Our Lord can say.

He gives us high mountains
To climb as best we can
Sometimes we badly stumble
As a mere, mortal man.

But, somewhere we find truth
Amongst bad lies and hate
Then look forward to meeting
The angel at God's golden gate.

We all may have struggled
In our life, here on His Earth
But His way is to test us
Preparing for heavenly rebirth.

So be gracious, and willing
In all that you might do
Our Lord will be watching
All your life, over you.

Maureen Westwood O'Hara

Love's Lost Sweet Dream

My world is spinning quicker and quicker,
and life seems little more than a flicker.

A candle flame that once burnt bright,
is now no more than a pale dim light,
of dancing shadows on the wall,
as it rises up, then down to fall.

And oh, how sad that life can be,
when love has turned away from me.

I toss and turn, I call your name,
but you are not there to ease this pain.

Oh where, oh where has my true love gone?
When into his arms I long to run.

And why, oh why, is life so cruel?
When it packs such a punch like a kick from a mule.

I love you now, as I'd loved you then
and silently whisper your name over and over again.

Oh please come back to heal this pain.

Deanna Southgate

Poor Mall

A distracted day
But in a hopeful way
Reason is reason enough.
A muggy stuffed-up air surrounds the bodies,
Milling about town
Escalators will flow side by side
Moving humans up and down
Spilling swarms out
Some rush with an agenda
Others cruise the tide of time
A real tree inside a shopping monstrosity echoing popular music
Billows through people.
Yes, a distracting day.

Lee Ford

A Victorian Splendour

A doll's house is my fantasy
  a miniature reside,
A house with my secrets
  lurking inside,
A Victorian splendour
  a house full of style,
It's a place where I wonder
  and dream for a while.

It's a house that's in miniature
  showing history and time,
It has hallways with grandeur
  and stairways to climb,
I'll be dining in splendour
  taking afternoon tea,
There's a grand library showing knowledge
  with leather books there to see.

A life lived in miniature
  a pretence of the past,
Living in luxury,
  in a house that is vast.
There are rooms to explore
  and places to hide,
A life that I seek
  and dream every night.

Dianne Audrey Daniels

KARMA

My darling pearl, I love you more
Than this poor soul can tell
You lived your life for me my dear
And I did give you hell
My gambling ways and women affrays
Did tear your heart apart
I beat you down and left you out
Whilst fun and fair I sought
Then in my prime I did decline
To note the warning signs
When on that day you came to me
With that funny little smile
You looked at me and I did see
Your eyes so full of tears and
That the children I had left you with
Had added many years
There you were all broken down
So old before your time
And I who had had so much fun
Did look so very fine
You came to me and whispered low
Your heart you would avenge
And then with one almighty blow
My own life you did end.

Susie Powell

Your Special Day

(Dedicated to Mummy)

As you wake on your special day,
The darkness seems to drift away.

Your smile gives the sun its warmth,
As the break of dawn appears,
Beneath the crimson mist.

Your love travels to all corners of the Earth,
As your eyes open and the doors to Heaven,
Are revealed behind the golden embers
Of night.

Your beauty gives angels flight,
As they sing in heavenly delight.

Amongst the wind, it calls your name,
Wishing you a special day.

Elysia Clarke (17)

Rainy Days

Every day I look outside,
And all I see is the rain out high
Dripping itself down the pipe
Watering plants until they're ripe

I look outside and all I see
A reflection of darkness inside me
Global disasters, what a pain
The rain, like tears, nothing gained

Teardrops falling down so quiet
Everyone stops all that riot
The rain like teardrops comes to fall
The rain like teardrops comes to fall.

Sheun Oshinbolu (12)

Cold Mountain Wind

Cold mountain wind,
Listen to my plea.
Take me in your arms.
Wind yourself around me.
Ensnare me in your grasp.
Thrash against my skin.
Burn into my soul.
Weave your strength inside me.
Rush through my swirling veins.
Numb all the aching.
Trap the pain escaping.
Freeze my broken heart.
Turn my tears to ice, and
Coat my spirit in frozen sadness.
Seep through me.
Control me.
Freeze me.
Numb me.
Beat me until I can feel no more.
Cold mountain wind,
Help me.
That is all I ask.

Amy Gillespie

TRUE FRIENDSHIP

(For Jane)

True friendship is just like a rainbow
It cannot be bought or sold
And when you're with that special person
Its many roads are paved with gold

In times of darkness and despair
When tears can fill the ocean space
Your special friend will come along
Bringing a rainbow of colours to your face

As friends you travel your chosen way
Hidden behind life's normality
Secure in the knowledge that just ahead
Someone waits, like a rainbow in tranquillity

On occasion when disagreement causes pain
Affecting all around in consequence
True friends try hard to heal the wounds
And hurt, like a rainbow, has no permanence

No matter the length of the journey
Nor the intimacies shared between friends
Like a rainbow all the magic and mystery
True friendship achieves and transcends.

Sandra Griesbach

Nonsense Illniss Or Taking The . . . Mick

Being ill is bad fer yer 'ealth, yer'd better be careful, it creeps up by stealth!
One day yer well, next day yer sick, it really can catch yer, far too quick.

Yer goes to the doc when yer not at yer best; 'e says, 'Warra crock! We'll try out a test.'
'E gives yer a bottle and says, 'Go fill this, right up to the top with some clear yellow ****!'

They take out some blood and a lump of flesh too, sum up results, 'It's chemo for you!'
They fill yer wiv drugs every four weeks; so life carries on in troughs and in peaks.

'Drink five pints a day to wash it all fru;' means many a trip out to the loo.
Still even at night I don't often miss; when I rush out for, to do what a man has to do!

Five days on steroids to make yer face red; then there's the sickness to keep yer in bed,
Back o' your mouth, tastes like tin; ruins the taste of me favourite gin!

Week four and yer 'air starts ter drop; well I really didn't 'ave much of a crop.
Arms, chest, ears, eyes, legs, nose, all defoliate; yes down there too, Mam! One notices!

There's cracked lips and mouth ulcers; well not many, only about the size of a penny,
Fingers tingle, can't button yer shirt. Lift right arm, left shoulder 'urts.
Can't go fer a walk, left leg's got a rash; so back into bed I think I will crash.

Constipated, maybee runny, it really could be very funny, (for you)

Take orf yer trahsis, skin peels orf too; bright red chemicals go
straight fru.
We'll fergit the rest, it's all rather bizarre; no immune system is one
step too far.

The treatment I'm told is of good use. If there's work ter be done
I've got an excuse.
I'm tired again I'm off ter rest. Or doze in the armchair, perhaps
that's best.

And now at long last, appunto seven I find I am here nearly in Heaven.
The doctor says, 'You're in remission' and to rejoin the choir
gives permission.

I can sing with choir, not lounge by t'fire.
But I ain't worbled fer many a day! While they've all practised
the winter away.
They say these drugs affect the brain, if I remember the words,
I'll fergit the refrain.
Besides, they all know every word! Now that really is absurd!

So I'll just mime, some of the time,
And when tenors sing their top 'C' note, I'll take time out and clear
me froat.
And when Conductor wants a short 'S' on his 'hiss',
I'll just leave the stage for a good healthy . . . *rest.*

Brian Reynolds

Stiff Upper Lip

When every day is a struggle
To reach the goals I have to meet
I say to myself most sincerely
'No, I must not quit.'
For every hurdle that I jump over
Along that long and rocky road
I know I must keep a stiff upper lip
Because, 'No, I must not quit.'
When each day brings a new worry
That invades my already-full mind
I bring right back that stiff upper lip
And say, 'No, I must not quit.'
At last the day has arrived
To the future I can now see
I take a look back to that stiff upper lip
And say, 'No, I never did quit!'

Margaret Ward

God Amongst Men

This perpetually reticent man, as whatever he may be,
an incandescent vein of light paving the way in the gloom of the night,
or dark of cloud and gathering rain,
the weight of a blessing on the branch of a tree.

Watchfully the man remains,
tempestuous weariness set in his eyes
yet sorrowful sights do not restrain
the strength in his bones on which faith relies.

His creation is now undeniably his,
his in its beauty,
its love and its passion,
and his in its ugliness,
its burning fire and blinded eyes.

There is no one with him now,
he is alone with his world.
Caressed and nurtured by the swallowing dark,
Ushered and guided by choral silence.

Snatched sensations visit his mind and such curious occupations,
as the vicious animal opening its skin, digging its own grave,
and the ceaseless, spiralling fall, of a teardrop in a tidal wave.
This defeated cry from aching eyes falls not for itself,
but for the severed touch of another,
from the nourishing eyes of a bloodless mother,
to fall atop her child's head,
branding the skin and burdening the air
with the searing fire and weight of the dead.

An eternal adornment to set his brow,
a melancholic scar upon his face,
no duplicitous arms must he shoulder now,
with this forget-me-not of warm embrace.

Ross Kane

The Flowers Of Romance

You sent me back the flowers,
that I had sent the week before.
The note said,
'They're dead now, I need more'
My hand went deep into my pocket
finding twenty pence,
oh, and a piece of fluff,
I found another pound in the vacuum
still I had not enough.
I needed to send you purple roses
with those green leafy things in-between,
plus a note saying, 'I love you'
I needed to seem real keen.
Instead of flowers I sent a note
about love and the prices of cars
I knew I had done right
I knew you had no vase!

Jonathan Harper

THE THREAD

Life is like a reel of thread -
Starts off full and plenty
Suddenly a flaw appears -
Soon to be half-empty.
Should one snip the flaw away
Or leave it as it is?
This is the burning question
As one begins to quiz.

All is well or so it seems
As merrily we soldier on
Then suddenly a break appears
What course to take is what I fear!
Ah yes . . . a little join
Is what one would expect -
But as the gap goes on and on
We linger as we go along.
Not worth all the trouble
The thread is running out
As life's mileage catches up
The light goes dim and out.

Carole King

NEW SHOES

I go into the shoe shop
And take a seat
I remove my shoes
From off my feet.
For I have decided
To buy something new,
I say to the assistant
'I'm ready for you.'
I try some brown shoes,
They don't fit so well,
(If I wear them
My feet are sure to swell.)
Next, there's a black pair,
They look very neat,
But they are much too narrow
For my broad feet.
Buying new shoes
Is always a chore,
And I have to keep on trying
Several pairs more,
Till I find a pair,
That fits just right
They're not too big
And not too tight.
Of course they're not as comfy
As my old ones were
But then, everyone knows
New shoes, never are!

Alexis Ashman

Everyone's Pain . . .

Why . . . do you always make me your whipping boy?
Your scapegoat to blame when things go wrong.
I . . . your submissive little pooch,
I roll over and play dead on your command.
Have I no shame, no sense of pride . . .?
I have but I hide it away, for inside I have died
. . . Enough to take on everyone's pain and not feel anything.

Pam McCormack

AWAKENED HEART

Far better
It is
To have
Slumbered
Unaware
Than to
Have been
Awakened
By a
Fleeting kiss . . .
O love,
What torments
Await my
Fretfully
Awakened
Heart?

Alice Parris

Safe And Sound

In the quiet waters beneath my skin,
The softest gentlest love is found.
My heartstrings pull and tug at me,
For my babies, safe and sound.

I know no greater love than that,
Of the love to which I'm bound.
Inside my womb, warm and soft,
Are my babies, safe and sound.

My cheeks are flushed with rosy red.
My sorrows gone, my sadness drowned.
My health and happiness no less
For you my babies, safe and sound.

It's nearly time for you to go.
Your gentle feet to touch the ground.
I pray for you my darlings that,
You will remain, still . . . safe and sound.

Geoffrey Kemm

When He Was Mine

I've written so much
the words have no meaning.
All my thoughts of you
on the pages I'm reading
and all the lies on my bed
have been lies in my head.
Today I see your face
as clear as though you were here.
You've been here too much
and scarred my atmosphere.
What do I do now?
You're faded into yesterday
and all the dreams we made so real
softly fade away.
My tears are falling
on your image in my mind
and all the words I wanted to say
are shrivelling and dying inside.

He looks at me with the dead expression
of a photograph, in time
leaving the pain and bitter memory
of that day he was mine.

Carol Wheeler

In The Vegetable Garden

We share little Gem tomatoes:
Miniatures of blushing jade
Entwined with slack, rubbery knots.

They fit exactly
Between the bottom teeth
And the dome of the palate.
Tiny round treasures
You can roll on the tongue
Like a kiss.

I enjoy the little explosion of juice
In my closed mouth;
But you half-open yours
To spray me with scent!

Diane Frost

Felixstowe Beach

The shingle beach
is cold to the touch
hard on the feet
not easy to lie on
so we bring blankets
and a flask of tea
and there we sit
till the tide rolls in

At low tide
the children build castles
where the shingle gives way
to smooth, wet sand.
Skimming pebbles
they paddle in the sea
then trudge up the shingle
for a bite of tea

Fishermen say
the easterly wind
around these parts
is good for the fish.
All night they sit
with rods poised, in winter
patiently waiting
for the slightest pull
on the quivering line

The farthest point east,
this coastline is rugged
and unrelenting.
In winter you freeze
in summer, the north-east wind
coming straight off the water
can burn you
even on overcast days

Sometimes
on a summer evening
when calm blue sea
meets cobalt skies
and all you can hear
is a seagull's cry
this stretch of the coast
is a mystical place.
Timeless, ageless
a place that I love.

Greta Robinson

The Pain Still Lingers

When somebody close to you
Has oh, so sadly died
The pain will never leave
And so many tears I've cried
It's like an empty hole inside
An empty chasm so deep
I'll never feel happy again
Every smile is a giant leap
The pain it will always linger
Your wedding ring still on my finger
I cannot sleep tonight
I miss you more and more
But there is a gentle light
I remember your smile
And more tears pour
I am coming my love
To feel your tender touch once more.

Sarah Beck (12)

NOT WRITTEN IN THE STARS (SONNET)

Would you let me hold your hand within a
Wizened 'grandpappy' clasp; and from the land
Of Nod, step out to soar up hand in hand,
And land upon the glistening Milky Way!
Tread along and eagerly hear you say,
'I'll be the good fairy and with my wand
Take you to far-off constellations grand . . .'
Pegasus, Orion . . . their nebulae
And those of Stingray, Crab or Eskimo . . .
Southern Cross, and Corona Australis.
To spring back o'er Oz, land of Kangaroo,
To Big Dipper, or the Plough, and find Polaris
To be guided to your chill wintry snow
And I, the tropics below Centaurus.

Malcolm Henry James

Said The Bridegroom To His Bride

Come to me to be detested,
Don't be shy and have no fear!
There are joys to be ingested
In a draught of fiendish cheer.

I shall spite thee and ignore thee,
I shall squash you with disdain.
Thou shall taste the bile so nasty
Of vituperative refrain.

Come to me with eyes wide open,
See my glory to the full.
Sing my praise and be forgotten -
Clueless over thee I'll rule.

Stella Young

Futuristic Prayer

I see our future,
In an old man's eyes;
One aged dejection,
In this world of depression.

I see our future,
In young men's eyes;
Youths of this land,
With nothing to hand.

I see our future,
In a dying man's eyes;
He struggles with strife
A world losing life.

I see our future,
In a newborn's eyes;
Our next generation,
In this world of contention.

I see our past flicker
In this old man's eyes;
Mirrors of our future,
Till we heed to this wise.

C A Keohane

A Nothing Hand

I am not free
I am full of clouds
And my stomach bitches
It flaps and turns and says
You've got to do these things
Got to get these things
Straight
Got
Got to do this
Got to think straight
Got to think clear

But I tilt my head and scratch my balls
And come up
With . . . come

Up with a warm hand that will never be warm

A nothing hand.

David Beller

AUTUMN

Autumn, autumn, is the time to rejoice and not fear
When we know the signs that the next cold season is near.
The evenings are shorter and all the leaves change colour and fall
The welcome bird-life visitors leave and we cannot hear their call.
The crops are harvested and the ground is left bare
Walkers rejoice that footpaths can be trampled without a care.
Rowan berries ripen for the starlings and maybe the fieldfare
And there's plenty for all others to digest and share.
Each day of autumn seems to have a latent chillness
Not quite wintry but just the autumn stillness.
Autumn, autumn, please do not depart so soon
And so leave us with the winter gloom.

Peter Parbery

Optimystic

Stillness speaks, a hearty yield
get into the gap, the zero point field
pardon me for saying, parlance has shifted
maybe you're not sick, the road to being gifted

lucid dreams, viewing remote
ships in the night, floating of boats
snakes bring you down, a ladder to raise
life's on CD, the game still plays

ain't done too bad, for someone just wishin'
an OBE, nocturnal emission
stirring quantum soup, but it's the plot that thickens
whose the mirror's fairest, which of the whickens

avidly trying to help, positivity equals success
stanza or quatrain, whatever fits you the best
maybe I'll make Eden, even get off Scott-free
guardian watching over, they put their trust in me.

Mark Musgrave

MIDLIFE CRISIS

I went through a midlife crisis
I fell for a girl of sixteen
I was totally besotted
It was a sad sight to be seen

I was like a fly round a jam pot
I just couldn't keep away
Even when I wasn't with her
I dreamed of her, both night and day

I even spent all my money
Hoping I'd impress her somehow
She twisted me round her little finger
But I can only see that now

I took her to work where I worked
And problems I helped her to face
But I was the one with the problem
I was a hopeless case!

All that she ever wanted
Was a friend who would be there
But because of my midlife crisis
I hoped for a love we could share.

Now, I never see her
But if I did, I'd do it all again
Because having a midlife crisis
I believe is part of the game.

B Page

THE BATTLE

Alone, silent I look around,
Emptiness all around me, not a sound.
I try to speak but no words escape,
How I long to speak, to break the silence.

Anger fills my thoughts, it does not stop,
It consumes my happiness;
I try to scream, release the hatred, yet it does not.
It builds up inside, boiling away, it rises and rises,
I can feel it filling my body,
Cold, empty and dark.

Suddenly, I reach for my sword glistening in the fog,
The cold metal burns my skin as I draw it across my body,
It rescues me from my feelings, from the darkness inside.
Deep red pain drips down my body soothing my skin as it escapes,
Slowly moving, it crawls down and breathes relief as it reaches the floor.
I am free, I can breathe once more.
Relief.

I can speak but there is no one to listen.
I am alone, in this dark empty room.
Only my red anger for company.
I hold my sword tight for it will protect me.

The pain is over but I will soon heal,
The feelings will return, the silence will remain.
I am not free; I am trapped in my prison of emotion.
Nowhere to go, nowhere to hide.
Alone I face the world, scared and small.

I wear my cuts with pride,
Medals of a battle fought and won.
I am ready for my next battle, I know I will triumph.
I know I will survive this war,
My war with me.

Wendy Dutton

Spirits Of The Night

Thick fog grows around the house,
The dead rise from their grave
Their spirits are starting to rouse
What could it be that these spirits crave?
It might be the blood of the living
Or to eat the fruit of the land
Maybe they aren't forgiving
We who are alive don't understand.
Should we stay and fight or run for our lives?
They draw closer to the house
Stay and see who survives.
Be a man and not a mouse.
The truth is coming, this I dread
For these spirits don't know that they are dead.

Andrew Ball

THE MOON

The moon hangs in the sky
As if hovering in time
Mystical as a wisp
Magical as the tides of time

Romantic, always romantic
Shining light pure and flawless
Upon us as we stand and stare
Dreaming of what could be maybe

Each night's a virgin moon
That graces us in the sky at night
Perfectly unblemished innocences
Gently crossing the heavens

Lighting a path to guide us solely
As we're lost in thoughts and time
Wandering uncertainly through our lives
Wrapped in thoughts of this and that.

The moon.

Carole A Cleverdon

Moments Of Peace

Quiet moments
By quiet waters,
I feel quiet moments of peace.

Let my soul drift
Across the water,
As it quietly bathes.

Secrets of this golden hour
Are subtly
Hidden beneath.
Not that my body
Can discover them.

Only my soul can feel these
Quiet moments of peace,
Now holding me still.

And the power
From this secret,
Fulfils my need to live.

Benvenuta Di Bartolomeo

By Jove!

Come live with me and be my love:
I really am a handsome cove;
To share my home you'll have to move.
    As I live near the port of Dover,
    I often use the craft that hover
    Above the sea like dove, or plover.
Covered with gifts my love I'll prove;
We'll sing together like larks above;
Over the countryside we'll rove.
    I'll not treat you like a sloven:
    Never tie you to stove or oven -
    Around you all my dreams are woven!
Tarry no longer, love, in Hove:
Wear the lovely gown you wove -
It will fit you like a glove!
    Leave your coven, the witch's hovel,
    We'll write together our love novel:
    Our treasure trove will need a shovel!
We'll be as happy as pigs in clover;
So, call the furniture remover:
Please live with me and be my lover!

Dorothy M Parker

When Me Heart Goes Flying

When He makes the clouds rise from the ends of the Earth
When He sends lightning with rain, and brings out the wind
from His storehouse
It overfills me with confidence and joy
Inexpressible, irrepressible joy
As though me heart were going to fly off in space!

Don Best
Santarém, Brazil

THE GOLDEN

'Tis a pleasure to be here
On Bill and Mabel's 50th year
What a record they have set,
Fifty years since they met
That little church in Donaghmore,
Where Bill wed Mabel, his adored
A special bond was made that day,
To love, honour and obey.

A boy and girl, God gave them,
Fiona the girl and the boy named Glenn
Just over in France, Glenn teaches today,
'Bonjour Mum and Dad!
Happy Anniversary!'
Fiona the daughter, sweet as a rose,
Runs 'Country Capers', flowers she knows.

Family ties are close and rightly so,
Mabel's the anchor, everyone knows
What is your secret of married life,
Notching up fifty years as husband and wife?
I can only guess, 'it's forgive and forget',
Tell me later, I've a bit to go yet.

Bill's a crack shot, no one can deny,
Mabel, the target, he aimed sky-high,
At Articlave they do reside,
Earning a rest from patients' bedsides
For nursing was their daily bread,
But now retirement looms instead.

Time is precious to us all,
So Bill and Mabel have a ball!
The spark is there, it's not gone out,
So get up and twist and shout!
This is your 'golden day'
Celebrate it your way
Three cheers for Bill and Mabel,
Hip hip hooray, hip hip hooray, hip hip hooray!

Happy 50th anniversary!

Edwina McFarland

MOMENTS THAT JUST ARE

Who knows what will be, do you, do I?
For what of tomorrow? Life passes by so quickly.
Yet an hour can pass by so slowly,
every second can seem like an eternity, for the time to elapse.
The seasons come and go and the world revolves once more,
winter fades and gives way to the spring,
the herald of lazy summer days, that slowly fade away to
the rustic autumn tints, that mirror your life.
This is the way it will always be, for you to mourn the
many passing hours lost to the tides of time,
of which so certainly are and will always be your fate.
Always stopping to question and reminisce,
as the past is a place you can always go to.
Your reflections upon this life are influenced by your past actions,
carried by your persona, on through to influence tomorrow
the oncoming day that has yet to exist.
Are we the 'flotsam and jetsam', lost in amongst the stagnating
pools beside the signs of life's ever-busy highway,
Living a half-hearted, pseudo existence?
For what of the impatience of your youth?
The ideals, principles, everything that you were about,
but now the fire has died and your days of glory will be no more.
Regrets permeate the air; this hangs heavily upon you
as though it were made of lead.
The mirrored images cast by you upon the embittered-stagnated-waters.
Casting doubts upon all that was in your life,
influencing all that may yet come to be?
As you await that elusive second chance, to start over anew,
To start out upon a journey, a journey upon the tides of the soul?

Jonathan Covington

NEWSPAPER DELIVERY

Stand by your beds
Paper deliverers are on their way
To fill our heads
With knowledge of *Today*

Our customers arise with alarm clock chimes
Their *Sun* in disguise wrapped up in the *Times*
They plough through the snow, my God, it's a faff
But you all get through with the *Telegraph*

They're prompt on the dot
And dressed to impress
Our customers who cannot
Collect their *Express*

Boys and girls, you're all a *Star*
For keeping the service right up to par
You're the tops, the best there has been.
You can all equal *Times Fin*

Your timing is impeccable
Straight on the nail
Your promptness infallible
For delivery of the *Mail*

Boys and girls we thank you
For *Independent* and true
Guardian of the 'papers'
And magazines too.

Wendy Kirk

Tracy

As the princess sleeps beautifully,
Tracy was my friend, a happy girl of the world,
Where love, song and laughter came naturally,
To the Queen of the Earth.

Dark and mysterious her Scottish and Italian birth,
Tracy is a woman of beauty and worth,
Who will be sadly missed by all,
But Heaven has Tracy now with angels at her side.

With peace and love she sleeps peacefully above,
Within a beautiful heavenly garden she keeps,
Where fairies complement her life,
With every beautiful flower growing sedately.

With hues of gold, purple, orange and red,
With blues, greens and yellows,
She holds the heavenly stars above her head,
With a silver-gold spear by her side, she said.

It is with love to her children, Lucy and William,
She watches over you with so much love and care,
And Socks the cat, whom she adored,
And Rita and Billy and sisters too.

Your life was precious my love,
No one can understand but God,
Now you are free as the birds in the tree,
Come softly my darling, singing to me.

One day we shall meet again,
United in Utopia's land,
Where love is openly spoken,
To a beautiful woman, we cherish you Tracy.

To the end of our time,
The beauty in you is extraordinary,
Like that of a poet's rhyme,
May God keep you softly, my love, forever more.

James S Cameron

Our Life

Our life is like a string of lots of various events
Passing quickly like in a colour movie
With a man jumping in and out of it
Trying to properly fit in all the time
Just stop, man, and look at it -
At the gorgeous nature around yourself
And you'll certain feel more happy then -
Just because you simply have it.

Vineta Priedite

THE SANDS OF TIME

Deserts upon deserts,
Making up the graves of time,
Nobody here for nobody dares,
Enter these sands of crime.

Consumed souls of time fading from colour
From the painted rainbow up in the sky.
Fading away, to the grey of the grave,
Although the dead did not really die.

The sands of time coloured crimson-red,
By the scalding scarlet sun,
And all of life who enter here,
Shall not be granted their time to run.

For once the sands are out of sight,
Don't ever think you have the right,
To stand upon the empty desert,
And continue to fight your ever-lost fight.

You must face the sun in the desert sky,
However much it may burn,
No matter how many blistering scars,
Once time has gone, it will never return.

Sarah Heptinstall

A Plant To Grow

A person of dreams is what I need
To know every plant that grows from the seed
He took a chance but was it wrong?
He will still grow when we're all gone

A man's ambition is to live his life
Live for the moment but beware of the knife
And count to three then make that wish
Your dream comes true of your final kiss

A memory to keep is a collection in your mind
To realise there is more than this mankind
To pass to the other side can it be tragic?
If so, wave your wand like you have magic

So the rain shall fall this sunny day
So you can still grow, come what may
Reach out your roots so you will grow
Ignore the weather when it starts to grow

8pm, it's not too late
To start anew, just wipe the slate
Every person has a chance to grow
Don't hide away, let it show

Take a chance and pay the price
Don't hide away and let us hear your cries
Stand tall and shout out loud
For you are making yourself proud

Victory comes with lots of glory
And please tell this poem as a story
A plant has to grow to let it show
Don't hide away, don't let it go.

Ian Connor

DANCE FOR ME . . .

Dance you sweet girl,
And don't look afraid,
Show them all, of what you're made.

Smile so bright,
Dear, don't you dare frown,
Don't let them know, that I let you down.

What will they think
Of that tear in your eye?
Wipe the damn thing, before you cry.

It is I who destroyed you.
I tore you apart.
Dance for me girl, it'll help heal your heart.

Kris O'Donnell

ZERO TO GAIN

To lie beneath the sun that shines
Where do we go from here?
To scramble up the wall of life
Or live a life of fear?

The sands of time just keep on falling
Within each eye that bleeds
And poets gone; I hear them calling
For love that each soul needs.

The rusted key lies on the floor
But I must turn away
The entrance has gone for evermore
Though I still search from day to day.

A friend turned up to help me out
But failure lay in store
A whisper turned into a shout
So I won't bother anymore.

Lee Connor

Love . . .

Love grows like an apple tree
Full of life, so wild and free
Love shines like a sun in motion
Alive for all, across each sea and ocean
Love can be a day of pleasure
But remember the pain, with the leisure
Love is always there so come what may
As you watch it grow, day by day
Love means happiness for everyone
And that is why it is never gone
Love will be here forever
For I know we'll always be together
Love between us feels so true
So please don't break my heart in two.

Graham Connor

As

Hey Gyp!
What lad?

Hmm . . . let me think it,
Why do I cry?

Try to remember lad,
Just like your dad,
But as regards Paula,
Well, she used to be smaller
Than she is now.

John Binns, (The Bearded Bard)

TEARS

A tear to fear
Is one that drops to your heart
It flows in your blood
To pain you all over.

A tear to cheer
Is one that seeps with a laugh
As it rolls down your cheek
It meets a happy mouth.

Andrew John Stevenson

My Dad

Wish I'd found time to talk to my dad.
About his life, he once had.
About his days, where he went to school.
Was he good, or did he break the rules?

About his youth, what he did as a boy.
If his life was good, and full of joy.
When he left school, and ran away from home.
Though he'd become a man of his own.

Joined the army and went to war.
It was all for us, he was fighting for.
Spent weeks in the trenches, guns all around.
Cold and wet feet, stuck in mud in the ground.

Never knew just how long they had got.
Getting away, without being shot.
Must have been hard having no food.
Frightened to stand, or even just move.

It was the First World War, so few survived.
But luck was with him, he came out alive.
He must have had many a tale to tell.
How they ducked and dived to miss the shells.

I wish he'd talked about the war.
I think he felt, he was being a bore.
Maybe telling was too hard to bear.
Only he knew, because he was there.

If he was with me here today,
I'd want to know, not walk away.
To tell me stories about the war,
And what they all were fighting for.

He was a hero, which makes me sad.
I wish, I'd found time to talk to my dad.
When he went, his stories went too.
Part of his life that I never knew.

Joan Morris

Hidden Cries

This helpless feeling inside me
Remains here, no strength to ignore
My conscience isolated
I'm not listened to anymore
My veins won't ease frustration
My thoughts trap in my mind
My body aches of anger
Relief so far behind
My existence irrelevant
Eyes need not to see
Nose needs not a scent
Mouth needs not to breathe
Continuous breakdown
I'm aware it's no phase
I'm alone and tired of exhausting days
Won't you hide my scars?
Won't you hear my calls?
My head buries in my hands
My nails scratch down walls
I feel collapsed on the ground
And my bones are so weak
I am battered and fallen
And considered a 'freak'
I am losing myself, my heart without choice
Tears roll from these eyes
Needn't speak with my voice
Can't define these emotions, to you I'm all lies
My suffering, bleeding, my constant cries
I've concerning visions that repeat in my head
My brain filled with such hatred in things I have said
Must I plead for that smile once expressed many ways?
Must I plead for my sanity, positive days?

I portray my distress; I've lost faith without thought
I'm no longer so fearless, for I am distraught
I must leave me behind and just end this instead
I am bruised and defeated, I am broken, I'm dead.

L S Young (15)

Anger III

The anger I'd thought,
So hard, to quell
Now flares anew.
As supplicant I'd come,
Not, as you suppose
To crave forgiveness,
But, to save a friendship
I found was fantasy;
For what, of substance,
Could founder on a thing
So frivolous, as a frown?
You asked if I thought
You cruel. No, not cruel.
For cruelty revels
In another's pain,
And that . . .
Requires empathy.

Rad Thomas

A Falkland Tribute

There is so very little we can ever say or do
    To repay devoted duty of those, that special few
They knew that when they stepped ashore,
    To give their best, their lives and more

For history made in that Falkland State
    Was conceived of principle, not one of hate
We read of Simon's battle against horrific odds
    But he remembers dearly his friends beneath the sods

We can wonder why and wonder when, what really should be done
    To replace those tragic givings in wars that can't be won.
We bow our heads in deep respect, perhaps it should be shame
    For everyone is someone, the difference is the name

Memories are for keeping, treasured are the best,
    But thoughts of hard-fought battles, seem better than the rest
Port Carlos was the water, in a cold and southern space
    Coveted by some others, of just another race

We should feel quite humble, go down on bended knees
    Thank God for all those heroes in graves that no one sees
Our thought must go to kinsfolk, to the kids they left behind
    For this is dedication, their gift to all mankind
Ignore the greed of others and hold our heads up in pride
    There never could be payment to all those men who died.

E F Croker

ASTRONOMY

In the park,
jeans on hips,
girls group at the edges
of youths chasing footballs
testosterone in their feet.

Small children join together
like links in a chain
on roundabouts,
envelop climbing frames,
centipede down slides.

Parents like me hover,
kick the ball back,
borrow the kids' fun,
keen as astronomers
keep looking for their childhood,
refuse to see the approaching eclipse
of middle age.

Andrew Button

Turnaround

I'm experiencing a complete turnaround,
Everything's tranquil, I'm feeling sound,
It's happening, the lights are switched on,
The sadness and heartache has finally all gone.
I am relaxed and I'm happy, you lifted my moods,
No emotional roller coaster, no dark interludes.
My heart is no longer racing, it is steadily beating,
The stress and the doubt is quietly retreating.
It is my own demons, I am defeating,
My grey matter's not ill, it doesn't need treating.
I am still in the woods but I can see through the trees,
I'm not living in terror, I can do as I please.
I'm walking tall, I have got off my knees,
I was locked in a cage and you found the keys.
I open my eyes, look up and see,
The love and devotion you are giving to me.

Madeline Morris

THE MOLE AND THE MOUSE

'Hello, Mole,'
'Hello Mouse, did I see you come out of that house?'
'Yes,' said the mouse, 'it was me
I've had to come out for some fresh air you see
Winter's tough for a mouse like me'
'Can you tell me how you get in?'
'It's easy enough, Mole, because I'm so thin
I shin up the drainpipe and in I go
A lovely warm house - and I lie low
The traps are out - but I'm hard to please
What they don't know is, I hate cheddar cheese
I rifle the cupboards to see what I can find
All packet stuff, it boggles my mind
I nibble and nibble and nibble my way through
Oats and bran flakes - they have to do
You see, Moley, it's a breeze
Ignoring those traps with that awful cheese
I go in and out whenever I please
I'm warm - I'm fed and sleep by the 'AGA' when I go to bed
Come the spring, I'll bail out
Back to the fields to roam about
There's only one hazard that I can see
It's the combine harvester - to come along and flatten me.'

Marilyn Hine

NOT FOR ME

I saw it on the screen one day
And felt the pain engulf my heart,
An icy stare bore straight at me
As reality hit - we were not to be.

Why he could not tell the truth,
And be up front with me?
I'll never know as I won't ask,
And he won't say, he's far away.

I promised myself all manner of things
Including not losing my heart,
But love has a way of seeping right through
He's with me today, and tomorrow too.

I see him every now and then
And the pain begins to ease,
I tell myself to 'lighten up'
He was nothing . . . 'just a tease'.

Janice Melmoth

A New Awakening

How still the earth
So cold and damp
Weep not, oh summer sun
For thou has warmed with tenderness
Our lives though now you're gone
How rich in mind
But sad in thought
How fast the year has flown
Swift as a bird upon the wing
No more 'twill be no more
Than fast upon another year
New hopes and dreams take shape
But cling in thought to days now gone
A new dawn will awake.

Mary P Linney

CHILDREN

There is a tightening, a filling,
And my belly is grown,
From the secret gestation
Of blood and bone.

I place wet fingers
In a fruiting womb, and with
A visceral slip or a hard labour
These children come.

I give birth to ciphers, cadences,
Songs and a river of sound
Then find myself breathless,
Seeing living forms.

I would hold these babies,
Lullaby them in my arms.
They would rest there humming
Never lost or spurned.

But they squeal to be out,
So full of themselves,
And how they secretly preen,
How they shake themselves open,

How they dance up
Lick themselves to a shine
Straining to be away,
Trembling to be seen.

J L Adams

My Lover

I miss your smile
I miss your touch
I miss the things
We used to love

I miss your laugh
I miss your tears
We shared them all
For so many years

I miss your love
You gave to me
And I miss the life
We used to have

I miss the things
We used to do
But most of all
I miss you.

Ella Wright

The Shoppers

The broken drone of gossip and the whine of conversation
Fills the air like smoke and drifts in wreaths of desolation,
Marking out the passage of the lonely and the tragic
To whom someone else's tragedy is equivalent to magic.

Dialogue is monologue; it's where the two combine
In shopping malls and busy streets where housewives pass the time
Of day; sad, secret intellectuals, misplaced presidents and judges
Take the stand and wrangle out their neighbours' fates
And others' private grudges.

Well-fleshed bodies, healthy faces, anorexic minds
Searching for an outlet for frustrations shared in kind;
The frustrations of the human soul deprived so much by life,
Disillusioned by the girlish dream of the status known as 'wife'.

Janet Mary Turner

Faces Of The Kingdom Centre

These are the many faces of the modern world.
Those bland, unsubtle masks which come and go,
On errands of fate or supreme irrelevance.
In shops and cafes, banks and pubs.
Some are the hands which steer important wheels.
Pen letters to a lover, or just good friend.
Even write upon the tablets of the nation's law.

They stroll between the broad facades
Of recent time's defensive tyranny.
Walking with care lest they touch the walls.
So pristine, blinding in the skylight's sun.
Theirs is the safety of the comforting throng.
Security in meeting old-remembered friends.
Thoughts on replacement curtains in the furnished room.
The three-piece suite that takes ten years to pay.
The wedding suit, blouse, shoes and hat.
To get the right length 'tween cuff and fingertip.

For them the moon has but an earth-turned side.
For them the world is small enough to know.
Friend's joke they cannot see, nor understand.
But laugh the same, him not to hurt.
Each longs for tropic's breeze that carries joy's caress.
The rainbow straddling both Lomond Hills, or how
To meet a payment looming soon.
Such thoughts lie dormant in each passing clone.

A Brown

Lambs To The Slaughter

They were all doing it so the rumour said,
had been for months with each flesh they met.
Degrees pinned to chests, the cool don't hold out.
They lower, go down, close eyes, and let

Anyone willing to have a cheap thrill
devour them breathlessly when and where they will.
At the cost of innocence and fading class,
a generation's self-respect is easy kill.

And now naïve bumps show and itches spread,
they think how easy the shepherd led
childhood to suicide in ten minutes or less
and how easy it would have been if they had said

No to the bullies, the 'trendy' flock,
of whom boast, try to grow too soon, and always mock.
Their attempts to mature in vain, there's proof.
Young lives ruined, that's the cold, harsh truth.

Rebecca Connery

Jon David

Very soon a grandchild new
Is it pink or is it blue?
At this time I have no clue
All I know is that it's due

Now I know it is a boy
A lovely cuddly bundle of joy
Laying there all sweet and coy
On me it will its charms employ

A life that I can help to mould
For him what does the future hold?
This treasure worth his weight in gold
How welcome he is to the fold.

Mary Jones-Barlow

Apple Blossom

I told you, I'd seen spring lambs,
I waited to see your face.
I heard laughter in the hall,
I'd lined up treats to take.
You sounded strange,
You didn't know.
You await the next set.
You never tell.

Sarah Evans

Ode To Modern Britain

They call it British radio and television, why?
They don't speak of a man these days,
He's just another guy.
I often wonder how they class this unsuspecting gent.
I always thought a guy was used for holding up a tent.

We can no longer watch a film as in the days of yore,
We have to watch a movie now,
It really makes me sore.
We can't go to the chemist, that's an out-of-date description,
A pharmacist is now the place to go for your subscription.

Now 'trick or treat' is creeping in, as well as bonfire night,
But now we're back to guys again,
I'm sure it isn't right.

We used to buy a yard of wood,
But now it's all in metres,
It's not a gallon now we get,
It's 'four point something' litres.

For years and years we struggled hard,
And put up quite a fight,
To try and get the 'powers that be' to keep our Fahrenheit
But no one took much notice,
Their decisions had been made,
And so we had to work out hot and cold in Centigrade.

But still they weren't quite satisfied,
They said, 'We want no fuss, we've had enough of Centigrade,
We'll call it Celsius.'

We used to build the finest ships,
Our steel was unsurpassed.
We sold our wool throughout the world,
Our cars were built to last.

We fought to raise the lowest wage
To keep up with our neighbour,
But now we buy from foreigners,
Who only use slave labour.

With one thing and another
I'm getting pretty vexed.
I wonder what the flipping heck,
They're going to think of next?

Brian Ellis

If It Could Only Be

If it could only be for all of us to be free.
Giving love to all, help for those in despair.
What joy there would be, the world a better place
For each and every one.
Creed or colour matter not.
God's love and grace spread among us all.
No more dark shadows linger, elation in our hearts.
Children full of childish glee.
The old and impaired eased from their daily torment.
Illness banished.
Please God hear my humble plea.
Let it be.

Norman Andrew Downie

A POEM UNLEASHED

Silence is the loudest sound,
As I cast my thoughts around.
Pictures in my mind abound,
But ideas fall on stony ground.

Once I'd write with unseemly haste,
All that's left is a desert waste.
On my lips the words I can taste,
With pen and ink they can't be traced.

My mind is lost in swirling fog,
With feet stuck fast in peaty bog.
Tired I sit down on a fallen log,
And pat the head of a passing dog.

Has my brain burnt itself out?
Surely not, I give a pout.
A tiny seed begins to sprout,
The wait is over and I shout.

I scribble with a frenzied burst,
Thank goodness I'm no longer cursed.
I've worked up an almighty thirst,
This poem unleashed is the first.

Rosemary Davies